Human Resource Development in the Organization

MANAGEMENT
INFORMATION
GUIDE : : 35

Human Resource Development in the Organization

A GUIDE TO INFORMATION SOURCES

Jerome L. Franklin

Vice President and Senior Associate
Rensis Likert Associates, Inc.
San Diego, California

and

Adjunct Associate Research Scientist
Institute for Social Research
University of Michigan, Ann Arbor

GALE RESEARCH COMPANY · BOOK TOWER · DETROIT, MICHIGAN

Library of Congress Cataloging in Publication Data

Franklin, Jerome L
   Human resource development in the organization.

   (Management information guide ; 35)
   Includes indexes.
   1. Organizational change—Bibliography. 2. Manage-
ment—Bibliography. I. Title. II. Series.
Z7164.07F72   016.6584'06   76-28289
ISBN 0-8103-0835-5

VITA

Jerome L. Franklin is currently vice-president and senior associate of Rensis Likert Associates, Inc., and adjunct associate research scientist at the Institute for Social Research, University of Michigan. He received his B.A. in economics from the University of California, Berkeley, and his M.A. and Ph.D. in organizational psychology from the University of Michigan.

Franklin has authored and coauthored monographs and professional articles in the field of organizational behavior and organizational development. Two of his monographs include SURVEY-GUIDED DEVELOPMENT I: DATA BASED ORGANIZATIONAL CHANGE (with D.G. Bowers) and SURVEY-GUIDED DEVELOPMENT III: A MANUAL FOR CONCEPTS TRAINING (with A. Wissler and G. Spencer). Articles have appeared in various journals including ADMINISTRATIVE SCIENCE QUARTERLY, JOURNAL OF CONTEMPORARY BUSINESS, MICHIGAN BUSINESS REVIEW, and the JOURNAL OF APPLIED BEHAVIORAL SCIENCE.

CONTENTS

Contents

INTRODUCTION

The materials in this bibliography focus on the enhancement of organizational performance and individual well-being through the development and improved utilization of human resources. This emphasis on the social and psychological facets of organizational functioning is encompassed by a field often referred to as organization--or organizational--development (OD).

Organization development is a comparatively new area of exploration and practice. Although its roots may be traced back as far as the first attempts to improve the performance of organizations, systematic research in this area has appeared with frequency only within the past ten to fifteen years.

Of greater consequence than its history is this field's actual and potential impact on individual lives and institutions. This impact appears enormous and is expanding at an astounding rate. Organizations of all types are gaining experience with OD activities. Major schools across the country offer courses in the area. Academic institutions and private organizations teach additional seminars. Consultants offer a multitude of services aimed at improving the quality of individual working life and organizational performance.

This field is flourishing for a number of reasons. A few are immediately obvious. There is the constant pressure for managers to improve the performance of their organizations to survive in a competitive world. This need is characterized by both a desire to correct obvious problems in organizational functioning, such as a decreasing quality or output of the service or product, and by pressure to improve already good situations.

Significant pressure for the expansion of this field also has arisen from those active in developing and applying the various techniques associated with organization development. Books and articles, training materials, and consultant services all add to the pressure for managers to become involved in OD activities.

The most important pressure toward an increase in OD activities may be current social concern about the quality of work experiences. There exists considerable social pressure to minimize negative effects (or maximize positive effects) of work experiences while also improving the outputs from organizations. The values inherent in these goals are precisely those espoused by the proponents of organization development. Essentially, the dual benefits of individual well-being and organizational performance are the cornerstones of the field of organization development.

It should be noted that the field includes considerable controversy. In fact, the content and boundaries of the field are debated, as well as the value of activities which it proposes. The literature does not provide clear insights about the limits of the field. The current trend is to include almost everything conceivable. It is also unclear which activities included in the area are truly beneficial. Some critics call for more careful evaluation of the results of organization development efforts. An examination of the literature supporting the usefulness of OD activities serves to justify this concern. Although good research and documentation exist, they are rare, and, as often as not, they indicate problems and negative consequences resulting from OD activities.

Thus, organization development is a young and growing area. In the long run it may grow into a hardy field based upon solid theory and practice. Currently, however, OD is characterized by a great deal of activity which often appears to exist without the presence of clearly understood goals or precisely defined sets of activities.

Included in this bibliography are books, book chapters, reports, and articles representing diverse views, but sharing some commonalities. Most of the references are recent contributions. More than half were published in the 1970s, and nearly all were published after 1960. This chronological selection represents both the flurry of recent publications and the author's judgments concerning the durability of most of the older pieces.

Much is being written about organization development, but new knowledge is painfully slow to emerge. Most of the literature repeats what has been said previously--much of it simply folklore--or provides personal experiences testifying to the virtues of one or another OD activity. Knowledge emerging from solid theory or well designed and executed research represents an extremely small percentage of what has been published. A positive note must be sounded, however, since knowledge in this field is expanding. In fact, one problem encountered in assembling this bibliography was the constant temptation not to finish because potentially significant pieces were continuously appearing.

Purposefully excluded from this bibliography are publications which are not readily available in journal, book, or report form (e.g., symposia papers not published elsewhere), and superficial accounts of personal experiences which were judged to offer little in terms of advancing the state of the field.

This bibliography has been organized in three major divisions: (1) Organization

Development: Background and Overview; (2) Development Strategies and Techniques; and (3) Case Studies. Abstracts of each book, chapter, report, and article contain summary descriptions of the major ideas and a listing of major topics. Where appropriate, the abstracts also include contents and a listing of contributing authors. Materials within each subsection are arranged according to the alphabetical order of authors. Author, title, and subject indexes are included to facilitate the rapid location of materials.

Several individuals provided valuable assistance in the preparation of this bibliography and an earlier version published through the University of Michigan's Institute for Social Research. Typing and editing of the previous monograph were done by Cindy Bunt, Jane Delaney, Carrie Lewis, Carol Shirley, Edie Wessner, and Anne Wissler. The tasks of typing and organizing this book were skillfully performed by Jane Delaney and Barbara Wank. The editors of the JOURNAL OF APPLIED BEHAVIORAL SCIENCE kindly granted permission to include materials from that source, and the Institute for Social Research permitted the inclusion in this book of materials previously appearing in a bibliographic monograph entitled ORGANIZATION DEVELOPMENT: AN ANNOTATED BIBLIOGRAPHY (1973). I wish to express my appreciation to the institutions and individuals cited above for their contributions to this effort.

Jerome L. Franklin

Section 1

ORGANIZATION DEVELOPMENT: BACKGROUND AND OVERVIEW

This first section of annotated references provides materials broad in scope and of particular value for understanding both the roots of this field and key elements of organization development as it now exists. Five subsections have been established to organize these materials. The first includes background materials on the broad theoretical bases for this field. These materials have been separated by publication type into three categories: (1) books and monographs; (2) articles, book chapters, and major reports; (3) books of readings and collected case studies.

Materials in the second and third subsections focus on areas basic to the development of the field. The second subsection concentrates on attitudes, norms, and values and the third on group processes. A great deal of the literature emphasizes these themes.

The fourth subsection includes materials more directly concerning the practice of organization development. These works examine the roles of those attempting to implement OD efforts, as well as the issues of identifying problems and evaluating results.

The final part of this first section is devoted to literature reviewing both anecdotal and empirical reports which attempt to summarize their findings and to formulate generalizations about the field of organization development. Of these pieces the article by Leavitt (See p. 76) has been frequently cited as a valuable framework for understanding basic approaches to organizational change, and the Greiner piece (See p. 76) has served as a basis for understanding major phases and approaches to change. The compilation by Friedlander and Brown provides a more recent overview of the field (See p. 74).

GENERAL ORGANIZATION DEVELOPMENT THEORY

Books and Monographs

Argyris, Chris [A.]. INTERVENTION THEORY AND METHOD. Reading, Mass.:

Addison-Wesley, 1970. 374 p.

Argyris describes interventions in human social systems and presents case illustrations. Three basic requirements are suggested for effective interventions: the generation of valid information; the making of free, informed choices; and internal commitment to the choices made.

Behaviors leading to system competence are described. System competence itself is defined in terms of six criteria: (1) awareness of relevant information; (2) understanding by the relevant parts; (3) manipulability; (4) realistic cost; (5) leading to a solution that prevents recurrence of the problem without deteriorating; and (6) preferably increasing the problem-solving, decision-making, and implementing processes. The conditions necessary for achieving these criteria are presented.

In elaborating the advantages and disadvantages of mechanistic and organic research, the author expresses a preference for the latter.

Argyris sets forth those qualities he considers basic for effective activity on the part of the interventionist: confidence in his own intervention philosophy and an accurate perception of stressful environments with growth experiences. The interventionist behavior needed to produce effectiveness includes (1) owning up to, being open toward, and experimenting with ideas and feelings; (2) helping others to own up, be open about, and experiment with ideas and feelings; (3) contributing to the norms of individuality, concern, and trust; (4) communicating in observed, directly verifiable categories, with minimal attribution, evaluation, and internal contradiction.

Contents

2

Topics

Attribution
Commitment
Conflict/Conflict Resolution
Defensiveness
Diagnosis/Evaluation
Intervention
Manipulation
Mechanistic Research

Organic Research
Organization Entropy
Resistance to Change
System Competence/Effective-
ness
Termination
T-Group
Trust
Valid Information

_____. MANAGEMENT AND ORGANIZATIONAL DEVELOPMENT; THE PATH
FROM XA TO YB. New York: McGraw-Hill, 1971. 226 p.

One of the most prolific writers in the areas of management and
organizational development uses his experiences in three organizations to focus on the difficulties encountered in improving the quality of work life. A second theme provides "the professional consultant with suggestions on how to deal with some of these problems
or at least how to face them squarely and openly". (p. xiv). The
author notes: "The book is written for the line executive and for
the professional consultant or interventionist in organizational development" (p. xii).

Contents

1. Introduction
2. Organization A
3. Organization B
4. Organization C
5. Conclusions I: Top Management and Organizational Development
6. Conclusions II: Organizational Development and Effective Intervention

Topics

Confrontation
Consultant
Consultation
Feedback
Management

Norms
T-Group
Theory X
Theory Y
Trust

Beckhard, Richard. ORGANIZATIONAL DEVELOPMENT--STRATEGIES AND
MODELS. Reading, Mass.: Addison-Wesley, 1969. 119 p.

Beckhard presents a concise view of organizational development in
terms of goals, strategies, and conditions leading to success or
failure. Illustrations are made through a presentation of case studies
focusing on change in five different aspects of organizational life:
culture, managerial strategy, the way work is done, adaptation to
a new environment, and communication and influence patterns. In

addition, he explores four different types of interventions and a variety of possible contractual relationships between the organization and outside help.

Topics

Adaptation	Culture
Change Goals	Environment
Change Strategy	Influence
Communications	Intervention
Contractual Relationship	Management

Bennis, Warren G. CHANGING ORGANIZATIONS. New York: McGraw-Hill, 1966. 223 p.

The second part of this book, in which Bennis expands many ideas expressed in his previous writings (See p. 26), is of special relevance to organization development. Bennis states that present theories of social change are suitable only for observers, not for practitioners or participants. "They are theories of change and not theories of changing." Drawing on the ideas of Robert Chin, Bennis presents the necessary elements of a theory of changing.

Change agents are viewed as similar in the following ways: (1) acceptance of the centrality of work in our culture; (2) concern with organizational effectiveness; (3) focus on interpersonal and group relations as central factors in assessing organizational health; (4) interest in changing relationships, attitudes, perceptions, and values of existing personnel rather than moving people to other situations; and (5) taking of the roles of researchers, trainers, consultants, counselors, teachers, and, at times, line managers. In addition to these similarities, change agents have a set of normative goals, which include the following: improvement in interpersonal competence of managers; a change in values so that human factors and feelings come to be considered legitimate; development of increased understanding between and within working groups to reduce tensions; and development of more effective team management, i.e., the capacity for functional groups to work competently; development of more rational and open methods of conflict resolution; and development of organic systems.

The laboratory method is suggested as an important means for instituting desired changes in organizations. "Laboratory training provides the instrument whereby normative goals and improvements set forth by theorists and practitioners of organization can be achieved," Bennis notes.

The necessary elements for implementation are described in the following manner: The client-system should have "as much understanding of the change and its consequences, and as much trust in the initiator of the change as possible." The change-effort should be perceived as "being as self-motivated and voluntary as possible." The change program must include "emotional and value as well as cognitive [informational] elements for successful implementation." The change agent can be "crucial in reducing the resistance to change by providing consultation and psychological support during the transitional phase of the change."

Contents

Part One: Evolutionary Trends in Organizational Development
1. The decline of bureaucracy and organizations of the future
2. Democracy is inevitable
3. Toward a "truly" scientific management: The concept of organization health
4. Changing patterns of leadership
Part Two: Planning and Controlling Organizational Change
5. Applying behavioral sciences to planned organizational change
6. Planned organizational change in perspective
7. Change-agents, change programs, and strategies
8. Principles and strategies of directing organizational change via laboratory training
9. Some questions and generalizations about planned organizational change

Topics

Attitude/Attitude Change
Bureaucracy
Change Agent
Change Goals
Change Strategy
Conflict/Conflict Resolution
Democracy
Interpersonal Competence
Laboratory Training

Leadership
Management
Organization Effectiveness
Organization Health
Planned Change
Resistance to Change
Team Building/Development
Values

Bennis, Warren G., and Slater, Philip E. THE TEMPORARY SOCIETY. New York: Harper Colophon Books, 1964. 147 p.

Focusing on the family and larger organizations, the authors examine the impact of change and democratization as well as various styles of human relationships. "This book is an attempt to relate a few dimensions of modern society--democratic systems of social organization, chronic change, socialization, and interpersonal behavior--to place them in some temporal perspective and to try to envision future combinations" (p. ix).

Contents

1. Democracy is Inevitable
2. Social Change and the Democratic Family
3. Beyond Bureaucracy
4. Some Social Consequences of Temporary Systems

5. New Patterns of Leadership for Adaptive Organizations
6. The Temporary Society

Topics

Bureaucracy   Democracy
Change Forces   Leadership

Clark, Peter A. ACTION RESEARCH AND ORGANIZATIONAL CHANGE.
London: Harper & Row, 1972. 172 p.

Case materials are integrated with a presentation of major themes
and issues to examine the roles played by behavioral scientists in
planned organizational change.

Contents

1. Introduction
2. Research: One Kind or Many?
3. Approaches to Organizational Change
4. Case Studies
5. The Uneasy Partnership
6. Valid Knowledge
7. Collaborative Role Relationships
8. Intervention Strategies
9. Organization Context of Action Research
10. Focus, Strategy and Content
11. Privileged Access
12. Models of Knowledge Utilization
13. The Requirements of Future Research
14. Conclusions

Topics

Action Research   Managerial Grid
Bureaucracy   Participation
Change Agent   Resistance to Change
Change Strategy   Role
Collaboration   Sociotechnical Systems
Confrontation   Structural Change
Diagnosis/Evaluation   Team Development
Intervention   Technological Change

Dyer, William G. THE SENSITIVE MANIPULATOR: THE CHANGE AGENT
WHO BUILDS WITH OTHERS. Provo, Utah: Brigham Young University Press,
1972. 219 p.

This book attempts to explain and describe the essentials of personal and organizational change. The major concern is for helping
others to change in the direction of improved maturity, effectiveness, and satisfaction (p. ix). The family is used as the primary
context for discussion of the principles presented in the book.

6

Contents

Part I: Change Directions: The Personal Challenge
Part II: Barriers to Change
Part III: Change Directions: The Professional Challenge

Topics

Change Agent
Communications
Conflict/Conflict Resolution
Consultant
Feedback

Group Processes
Intervention
Role
Trust

Fordyce, Jack K., and Weil, Raymond. MANAGING WITH PEOPLE; A MANAGER'S HANDBOOK OF ORGANIZATION DEVELOPMENT METHODS. Reading, Mass.: Addison-Wesley, 1971. 207 p.

This volume is a handbook of techniques useful for various purposes in organizational development efforts. The techniques and a series of case studies provide a view of specific activities engaged in by managers and those facilitating organization development efforts.

Contents

Part One: Move Over!
What's Going On?
1. What people want
2. What's wrong with our organization?
3. A symptomatology of organizational illness and health
4. Organizational development
5. Plan of this book
6. To proceed
The Third Party
1. Two traditions
2. What a Third Party does
3. Qualifications of a skilled Third Party
4. The client and the Third Party
5. What sort of Third Party help do you need?
Part Two: Four Case Studies
Case 1. Reorganization of a retail chain
Summary observations
Case 2. A problem of customer relations in an aerospace firm
Summary observations
Case 3. The development of a teacher education program
Summary observations
Case 4. Revitalizing a division of an engineering company
Summary observations

Part Three: Methods
Meetings to Bring About Change
1. The manager's diagnostic team meeting series
2. The confrontation goal-setting meeting
3. The family group diagnostic meeting
4. The organization mirror
5. Force field analysis
6. Sensitivity training laboratories
7. Meetings for two
8. The family group team-building meeting
9. The intergroup team-building meeting
10. Life/career planning laboratory
11. Follow-through
Methods for Finding Out What is Going on
1. Questionnaires and instruments
2. Interviewing
3. Sensing
4. Polling
5. Collages
6. Drawings
7. Physical representation of organizations
Methods for Better Meetings
1. Chart pads
2. Going around the room
3. Critiquing
4. Subgrouping
5. The fishbowl
Methods for Changing the Quality of Relationships
1. Role playing
2. Getting acquainted
3. Hearing
4. Positive feedback
5. Making deals (out on the table)
6. Likes and reservations
7. Nonverbal encounters

Topics

Action Research
Change Technology
Confrontation
Diagnosis/Evaluation
Feedback
Goals (Individual/Organizational)

Interview
Management
Role Playing
Sensitivity Training
Team Building/Development
Third Party

Ginzberg, Eli, and Reilley, Ewing W. EFFECTING CHANGE IN LARGE OR-GANIZATIONS. New York: Columbia University Press, 1957. 155 p.

Ideas are presented concerning change in large organizations involved in the process of decentralization. The focus is on behavior change at the top level of the organization.

Topics

Change Processes
Communications
Decentralization
Feedback

Learning
Management
Resistance to Change
Threat

Hornstein, Harvey A., et al., eds. SOCIAL INTERVENTION: A BEHAVIORAL SCIENCE APPROACH. New York: Free Press, 1971. 597 p. This book contains an introductory chapter and six major sections. Each section includes introductory comments by the editors and selected readings focusing on a major strategy of social change.

Contents

Topics

Action Research	Management
Attitude/Attitude Change	Managerial Grid
Behavior Change	Participation
Change Processes	Resistance to Change
Conflict/Conflict Resolution	Sociotechnical Systems
Confrontation Meeting	Structural Change
Data Collection	Survey Feedback
Decision Making	Team Building/Development
Feedback	Technological Change
Individual Change	T-Group
Laboratory Approach	Value Change

Huse, Edgar F. ORGANIZATION DEVELOPMENT AND CHANGE. St. Paul, Minn.: West Publishing Co., 1975. 448 p.

This book purports to put organization development into an overall perspective--using a systems approach to describe the underlying concepts and assumptions of OD.

Contents

Chapter 1: Organization Development and Improvement
Chapter 2: Systems and the Change Process
Chapter 3: Organization Development: Theory, Values, and Approaches
Chapter 4: Change, Planned Change, and Action Research
Chapter 5: Systemwide Approaches to Organization Development-- I
Chapter 6: Systemwide Approaches to Organization Development-- II
Chapter 7: Individual/Organizational Interfaces
Chapter 8: Concern with Personal Work Style
Chapter 9: Intrapersonal Analysis and Relationships
Chapter 10: Other Approaches to OD
Chapter 11: The Organization Development Practitioner
Chapter 12: Organization Development: Past, Present and Future
Appendix I: Selected Readings
Appendix II: Selected Cases

Topics

Action Research	Laboratory Training
Change Agent	Management by Objectives
Change Techniques	Managerial Grid
Conflict/Conflict Resolution	Process Consultation
Diagnosis/Evaluation	Role
Encounter Group	Sensitivity Training
Feedback	Survey Feedback
Grid Organization Development	Survey-Guided Development
Group Processes	Team Building
Job Design	Values

Kuriloff, Arthur H. ORGANIZATIONAL DEVELOPMENT FOR SURVIVAL. New York: American Management Association, 1972. 275 p.

This book's four sections cover the background and basic concepts of organizational development, and a definition of organizational development in terms considered important to the line manager and the organizational development specialist; the major findings of the behavioral sciences pertinent to cogent application of the methodology of organizational development; management by objectives and self-control as a process for regulating the other systems of organization; and the management of human resources of the enterprise in a systematic and practical way.

Contents

A. Organizational Development: Background and Definition
  1. Organizational Development and Management
  2. Background of Organizational Development
  3. Organizational Development Defined
B. Behavioral Sciences in Organizational Development
  4. Gaining Entry to the Organization
  5. Technical Interventions
  6. Behavioral Interventions
  7. Intervention Techniques
  8. Sensitivity Training--The T-group in Industry
C. Management by Objectives in Organizational Development
  9. Updating Bureaucracy
  10. Methods and Techniques of Management by Objectives
D. Management of Managerial Resources
  11. Management Manpower Planning
  12. Staffing and Development
  13. Identifying Management Potential
  14. Environment and Organizational Performance

Topics

Bureaucracy
Change Agent
Change Strategy
Change Technology
Communications
Conflict/Conflict Resolution
Consultant
Consulting
Decision Making
Diagnosis
Entry

Feedback
Group Processes
Leadership
Management
Management by Objectives
Need Achievement
Sensitivity Training
Structure
Team Building/Development
Technology
T-Group

Lawrence, Paul R., and Lorsch, Jay W. DEVELOPING ORGANIZATIONS: DIAGNOSIS AND ACTION. Reading, Mass.: Addison-Wesley, 1969. 101 p.

Using concepts from systems analysis, the authors explore three interfaces with reference to organizational development activities.

"The criteria we use for determining whether a particular change
will lead to the development of the organization at any one or
all of these interfaces is whether the change will lead to either
a better fit between the organization and the demands of its en-
viroment and/or to a better fit between the organization and the
needs of individual contributions."

As was the case in a previous volume (see below), the manner by
which organizational members deal with conflict is emphasized as
a crucial aspect of organizational effectiveness.

They present a model that suggests the relative proportion of cognitive to emotional aspects of a change method decreases as the
change target shifts from one of modest to fundamental behavior
change.

Contents

1. Introduction
2. Concepts for developing organizations
3. Organization-environment interface
4. The group-to-group interface
5. The individual-and-organization interface
6. Conclusions

Topics

Behavior Change	Environment
Change Processes	Individual-Organization
Change Strategy	Interface
Cognitive Change	Organization-Environment
Conflict/Conflict Resolution	Interface
Emotional Change	Systems Analysis

_____. ORGANIZATION AND ENVIRONMENT; MANAGING DIFFERENTIA-
TION AND INTEGRATION. Homewood, Ill.: Irwin, 1967. 294 p.

The authors report a study of ten industrial organizations in three
environments. They compare more and less effective organizations
on the dimensions of integration and differentiation.

Integration is defined as "the quality of the state of collaboration
that exists among departments that are required to achieve unity of
effort by the demands of the environment." Differentiation is defined in terms of "the difference in cognitive and emotional orientation among managers in different functional departments."

These two concepts provide a basis for the development of a contingency theory of organization. The theory proposes that successful organizations in a relatively stable environment will not be
highly differentiated and will not include elaborate integrating
mechanisms. Successful organizations in rapidly changing environments, however, will be highly differentiated and thus will require
elaborate integrating mechanisms.

A central emphasis is given to the role of conflict resolution in organizations. The authors identified three distinct modes of actually handling conflict in these six organizations: confrontation or problem solving; smoothing-over differences; and forcing decisions.

Contents

1. Background and approaches to the study
2. Organizations in a diverse and dynamic environment
3. Resolving interdepartmental conflict
4. Environmental demands and organizational states
5. Additional perspectives on resolving interdepartmental conflict
6. High-performing organizations in three environments
7. Traditional organizational theories
8. Toward a contingency theory of organization
9. Implications for practical affairs

Topics

Collaboration
Conflict/Conflict Resolution
Confrontation
Differentiation
Environment

Integration
Intergroup Processes
Organization Effectiveness
Problem Solving

Likert, Rensis. THE HUMAN ORGANIZATION. New York: McGraw-Hill, 1967. 258 p.

Likert expands and elaborates the theory of organization presented in an earlier work (see below). Emphasized in this work are various management systems, especially "System 4." Also emphasized is the importance of human resources in organizations.

Contents

1. New foundations for the art of management
2. A look at management systems
3. Productivity and labor relations under different management systems
4. The interdependent, interacting character of effective organizations
5. Time: A key variable in evaluating management systems
6. Improving general management by better fiscal management
7. The need for a systems approach
8. Measurement
9. Human Asset Accounting
10. Achieving effective coordination in a highly functionalized company and elsewhere
11. The next step

Topics

Causal Variables	Intervening Variables
Communications	Leadership
Decision Making	Management
End-Result Variables	Measurement
Feedback	Productivity
Group Processes	Scanlon Plan
Human Asset Accounting	System Approach
Influence	Trust
Interaction-Influence System	

_____. NEW PATTERNS OF MANAGEMENT. New York: McGraw-Hill, 1961. 279 p.

Likert presents a theory of organization focusing on effective management practices. The theory is based upon an integration of social science research conducted primarily at the Institute for Social Research, Ann Arbor, Michigan.

At the core of the organization suggested as being most effective is a system of reciprocal influence between organizational levels. Likert states with respect to the development of such systems that "There is not a large body of systematic knowledge nor are there well-developed procedures for dealing with the problem of building the kind of effective interaction-influence system called for by the newer theory."

The importance of obtaining accurate measurements of critical variables is a central theme. Organizational improvement is viewed as partially the result of feeding back information regarding successes and failures through short feedback cycles.

Contents

1. Introduction
2. Leadership and organizational performance
3. Group processes and organizational performance
4. Communication, influence, and organizational performance
5. The effect of measurements on management practices
6. Some general trends
7. Effective supervision: An adaptive relative process
8. An integrating principle and an overview
9. Some empirical tests of the newer theory
10. Voluntary organizations
11. The nature of highly effective groups
12. The interaction-influence system
13. The function of measurements
14. A comparative view of organizations
15. Looking to the future

Topics

Communications	Interaction-Influence System
Conflict/Conflict Resolution	Interpersonal Skill
Decision Making	Leadership
Feedback	Management
Group Processes	Measurement
Human Resources	Performance
Influence	

Lippitt, Ronald; Watson, Jeanne; and Westley, Bruce. THE DYNAMICS OF PLANNED CHANGE; A COMPARATIVE STUDY OF PRINCIPLES AND TECHNIQUES. New York: Harcourt, Brace, & World, 1958. 312 p.

The authors draw heavily from the therapeutic model in formulating their conceptions of planned change. The role of the change agent and the relevant forces that support and resist change are emphasized extensively.

Contents

1. Our orientation to the phenomena of planned change
2. Diagnostic orientations toward problems of internal relationships
3. Diagnostic orientations toward problems of external relationships
4. Motivation of the client system
5. Various aspects of the change agent's role
6. The phases of planned change
7. Initiating planned change
8. Working toward change
9. The transfer and stabilization of change
10. Some unfinished business
11. The scientific and professional training of change agents

Topics

Change Agent	Diagnosis/Evaluation
Change Forces	Motivation
Change Phases	Planned Change
Change Processes	Resistance to Change

Mann, Floyd C., and Neff, Franklin W. MANAGING MAJOR CHANGE IN ORGANIZATIONS: AN UNDEVELOPED AREA OF ADMINISTRATION AND SOCIAL RESEARCH. Ann Arbor, Mich.: Foundation for Research on Human Behavior, 1961. 99 p.

The authors present a series of case studies together with several generalizations about major change efforts. The generalizations include comments regarding the extensiveness of the change effort, the effects of self-concept, feedback, the effects of group support, the "change catalyst" role, and involvement in problem solving as a motivator for change.

Contents

1. Preparing an organization for change: Case I
2. Establishing behavioral objectives of change: Case II
3. Maintaining change momentum: Case III

4. Completing and stabilizing changes: Case IV
5. Conference insights
   A new role: The change catalyst
   A new technique of involvement: The controlled explosion
6. Toward an understanding of the management of change

Topics

Change Catalyst
Change Goals
Change Processes
Feedback
Group Processes

Involvement
Motivation
Problem Solving
Self-Concept

Margulies, Newton, and Raia, Anthony P. ORGANIZATIONAL DEVELOP-
MENT: VALUES, PROCESSES, AND TECHNOLOGY. New York: McGraw-
Hill, 1972. 640 p.

This book is divided into five major parts and several subsections.
Each section includes the editors' comments and selected readings
reprinted from other sources.

Contents

Part One: Introduction
1. Organizational development in perspective
Part Two: The Components of Organizational Development
2. Key elements in organizational development
Part Three: The Process and Technology of Organizational Development
3. The collection of data
4. The diagnostic phase
5. Intervening in the system
Part Four: Emerging Issues in Organizational Development
6. Problems and challenges in organizational development
Part Five: Case Studies in Organizational Development
7. The practice of organizational development

Contributing Authors

Albanese, R.	French, W.	Mouton, J.S.
Argyris, C.	Golembiewski, R.T.	Mullen, D.P.
Barnes, L.B.	Goode, W.J.	Myers, M.S.
Beckhard, R.	Greiner, L.E.	Pondy, L.R.
Benne, K.D.	Hatt, P.K.	Seiler, J.A.
Bennis, W.G.	House, R.J.	Selltiz, C.
Blake, R.R.	Jacques, E.	Sheats, P.
Blansfield, M.G.	Jahoda, M.	Shepard, H.A.
Blumberg, A.	Kahn, R.	Sloma, R.L.
Bradford, L.P.	Lawrence, P.R.	Tannenbaum, R.
Cannel, C.F.	Lewin, K.	This, L.E.
Cook, S.W.	Lippitt, G.L.	Turner, A.N.
Davis, L.E.	Lippitt, R.	Watson, J.
Davis, S.A.	Loftin, B.P.	Westley, B.
Deutsch, M.	Lorsch, J.W.	Wilson, J.E.
Ferguson, C.K.	Morton, R.B.	

Topics

Change Agent   Intervention
Change Phases   Laboratory Approach
Change Processes   Managerial Grid
Change Technology   Motivation
Conflict/Conflict Resolution   Resistance to Change
Consultant   Sensitivity Training
Data Collection   Team Building/Development
Diagnosis/Evaluation   T-Group
Intergroup Processes   Values

Margulies, Newton, and Wallace, John. ORGANIZATIONAL CHANGE:
TECHNIQUES AND APPLICATIONS. Glenview, Ill.: Scott, Foresman and
Co., 1973. 161 p.

As the chapter headings listed below indicate, this 161-page book
covers a wide range of issues regarding behavior change in organizations. According to the authors, the book is designed to examine techniques drawn from applied behavioral science and considered useful in planned organizational change programs, present
these techniques so that both managers and advanced students of
administrative sciences have a clear understanding of them, examine the factors that determine intelligent choice among the various techniques, and present the theory underlying these techniques.

The volume includes brief descriptions of a variety of issues and
techniques, supported by examples, cases, and reference materials.
It concludes with a listing of six propositions about change processes but does not include supporting evidence for them.

Contents

 1. Introduction
 2. Critical Dimensions of Change
 3. Data Collection and Action Research
 4. Learning and Change
 5. The Laboratory Approach to Change
 6. Applications of Role Theory
 7. Changing Team Relationships
 8. Changing Intergroup Relations
 9. The Use of Internal Consulting Teams
10. Some Concluding Propositions

Topics

Action Research   Feedback
Behavioral Change   Laboratory Training
Change Strategy   Learning
Change Technology   Roles
Consultant   Team Building
Consultant Team   T-Group

Maslow, Abraham H. EUPSYCHIAN MANAGEMENT: A JOURNAL. Homewood, Ill.: Irwin-Dorsey, 1965. 293 p.

This volume is a journal of ideas recorded by Maslow, based on his experiences during a period of time spent at Non-Linear Systems in California. He touches on a great variety of topics related to the central theme of good psychological management.

Topics

Attitude/Attitude Change	Management
B-Values	Psychological Health
Creativity	Regression
Eupsychian Management	Self-Actualization
Group Processes	Self-Concept
Individual Growth	Synergy
Leadership	T-Group

Roeber, Richard J. THE ORGANIZATION IN A CHANGING ENVIRONMENT. Reading, Mass.: Addison-Wesley, 1973. 158 p.

This volume of Addison-Wesley's OD series examines the issue of adaptation to changes in the social environment. A basic premise of this book is that change is occurring toward a "voluntary society." The tendency towards greater self-determination challenges many basic assumptions of management. The author explores the implications of this challenge for changes in work relationships and patterns and the nature of jobs.

Contents

1. Hidden Futures
2. Continuous Revolutions
3. The Roots of Change
4. Increasing Wealth and Increasing Choice
5. Toward a Voluntary Society
6. Case 1/Allied Minorities: A Case of Organizational Change Triggered by Shifts in the Commercial Environment
7. Case 2/The International Oil Industry in the Middle East: A Case of Adjustment Within a Changing Political Environment
8. Breaching the Organization
9. Government Limitation
10. Redefining the Corporate Role
11. Social Change and the Manager: Enforced Change
12. Social Change and the Manager: Union Initiatives
13. Internal Pressures: Anticipating Change
14. Democratic Organizations

Topics

Adaptation	Environment
Change Forces	Unions

Rush, Harold M.F. BEHAVIORAL SCIENCE CONCEPTS AND MANAGEMENT APPLICATION. New York: National Industrial Conference Board, Studies in Personnel Policy, No. 216, 1969. 180 p.

This report examines the study of human behavior in social settings, with emphasis on behavioral science concepts as they evolve from theory to laboratory experiments, to developmental research, and finally to on-the-job applications in managing human resources. The theories and contributions of five of the most influential behavioral scientists--McGregor, Maslow, Herzberg, Argyris, Likert--and descriptions of three prevalent techniques--sensitivity training, Managerial Grid, Menninger Foundation seminars--are capsulized. Detailed descriptions are given of behavioral science applications in ten firms--American Airlines, Armstrong Cork Co., Corning Glass Works, Genesco, Inc., Hotel Corporation of America, Raymond Corp., Steinberg's Ltd., Syntex Corp., Texas Instruments Inc., and the Systems Group of TRW, Inc.

This report concludes with a selected bibliography of behavioral science theory and philosophy.

The author presents excellent summaries of the major ideas of the behavioral scientists included in the report. The descriptions of the techniques are also good but do not provide a complete picture of the techniques currently available.

Contents

1. The world of work and the behavioral sciences: A perspective and an overview
2. Behavioral scientists: Their theories and their work
3. Human behavior learning: Three approaches
4. Company experience: A survey and an analysis

Topics

Individual-Organization Interface	Need
Management	Science-Based Management
Managerial Grid	Sensitivity Training
Menninger Foundation Seminar	Theory X
Motivation	Theory Y

Schmuck, Richard A., and Miles, Matthew B., eds. ORGANIZATION DEVELOPMENT IN SCHOOLS. Palo Alto, Calif.: National Press Books, 1971. 264 p.

The editors have aimed this book at five specific audiences, for the purpose of spreading OD to the classroom and promoting scholarly research on the subject. The audiences are: (1) educational administrators, department heads, unit leaders, and teachers; (2) school psychologists, curriculum specialists, and counselors who in one way or another must deal with systemic variables; (3) state department of education personnel; (4) specialists working in regional educational laboratories; and (5) professors of education involved in the redesign of pre-service and in-service training programs as organizations and the dynamics of educational change.

The editors present nine recent studies of organization development in schools. They have preceded each chapter with brief comments on its most notable elements: its theory, technology, measurement methods, place in the literature, relationship to other studies, and unique features. The final chapter contains a summary and suggestions for further investigation.

Contents

Topics

Change Agent
Change Strategy
Collaboration
Communications
Conflict/Conflict Resolution
Confrontation
Consultation
Durability of Change
Encounter Group

Feedback
Group Processes
Interpersonal Processes
Power
Problem Solving
Role Playing
Sensitivity Training
Survey Feedback
T-Group

Schmuck, Richard A., et al. HANDBOOK OF ORGANIZATION DEVELOPMENT IN SCHOOLS. Palo Alto, Calif.: National Press Books, 1972. 436 p.

"This handbook is a guide to planned actions for facilitating human responsiveness and adaptability in school organizations" (p. xiii). Chapters include presentations of basic theory and intervention technology. Tools provided include instruments for assessing present and ideal exercises for stimulating the function, exercises for stimulating the function, and procedures for use during actual day-to-day work in the organization to attend to the function and improve it." In addition, chapters include suggestions for designing workshops and evaluating interventions and training designs.

Contents

Chapter One: Organizational Theory
Chapter Two: Organizational Training
Chapter Three: Clarifying Communication
Chapter Four: Establishing Goals
Chapter Five: Uncovering and Working with Conflicts
Chapter Six: Improving Meetings
Chapter Seven: Solving Problems
Chapter Eight: Making Decisions
Chapter Nine: Designing Training Interventions
Chapter Ten: Evaluation at Beginning, Middle, and End

Topics

Change Strategy   Group Processes
Change Technology   Problem Solving
Communications   Role
Conflict/Conflict Resolution   School
Diagnosis/Evaluation   Sensitivity Training
Entry   Survey Feedback
Feedback

Sofer, Cyril. THE ORGANIZATION FROM WITHIN; A COMPARATIVE STUDY OF SOCIAL INSTITUTIONS BASED ON A SOCIOTHERAPEUTIC APPROACH. London: Tavistock, 1961. 178 p.

The final chapter of this book concentrates on organizational change. Generalizations are drawn from experiences in three different types of organizations (industrial, medical, educational).

Contents

Part One: Three Case Studies
   1. An industrial setting: The Davidson Company
   2. A medical setting: The James division and research unit
   3. An educational setting: The Helmsley department of management and production engineering
Part Two: Theoretical Analysis
   4. Therapeutic and research components of the work
   5. Regularities and principles in social consultancy
   6. Processes of organizational change

Topics

Change Agent   Defensiveness
Change Phases   Diagnosis/Evaluation
Change Processes   Environment
Commitment   Leadership
Conflict/Conflict Resolution   Resistance to Change
Consultant   Structure

22

Taylor, James C. TECHNOLOGY AND PLANNED ORGANIZATIONAL CHANGE.
Ann Arbor, Mich.: Institute for Social Research, 1971. 151 p.

Taylor focuses on the level of technology as a critical variable in
efforts to gain approval of changes toward more participatory and
responsible activities in organizations.

The studies involve an analysis in various companies exposed to a
variety of change activities. Survey data were gathered at least
twice in each group studied.

The data indicate that "sophisticated technology . . . not only
will facilitate change efforts which are in a direction consonant
with that determined by the technology, but sophisticated technology will aid in resisting change efforts which are in a direction
opposed to that determined by the technology."

Topics

Resistance to change   Technology

Articles, Chapters, and Reports

Argyris, Chris [A.]. "Conditions for Competence Acquisition and Therapy."
JOURNAL OF APPLIED BEHAVIORAL SCIENCE 4, no. 2 (1968): 147-78.

Competence acquisition and therapy are defined as learning processes that are distinguished from each other on several key dimensions. They differ with respect to the individuals who can be
helped and the conditions deemed necessary for each to occur.
Competence acquisition focuses on the development of interpersonal
competencies. Therapy stresses survival.

"Competence acquisition requires psychological success, the giving
and receiving of information that is directly verifiable, minimally
evaluative, and minimally contradictory." Therapy requires "indirectly verifiable knowledge, knowledge that is evaluative and
can lead to psychological failure," the author writes.

Topics

Interpersonal Competence   Therapy
Learning

Barnes, Louis B. "Organizational Change and Field Experiment Methods." In
METHODS OF ORGANIZATIONAL RESEARCH, edited by Victor H. Vroom,
pp. 57-111. Pittsburgh: University of Pittsburgh Press, 1967.

This two-part chapter includes discussion of organizational change
in terms of approaches, relationships, and processes as well as a
review of field experiment methodologies useful in studying these
issues. The first part summarizes the following: (1) Leavitt's articles
(See p. 76) describing three approaches to change (people, structural, and technological); (2) Bennis's discussion (See p. 4) of change

styles other than "planned change" (indoctrination, technocratic, interactional, socialization, emulative, natural); (3) Greiner's identification ("Organization Change and Development." Ph.D. dissertation, Harvard University, 1965) of the most often used approaches to organizational change (decree, replacement, structural, group decision data discussion, group problem solving, T-group).

Individuals within organizations who support and resist changes are divided into four types based on these dimensions: Advocates, Resisters, Rational Objective, Emotional Subjective. The four types are defined as follows: (1) Rational Advocates are Advocates who are Rational Objective; (2) Radicals are Advocates who are Emotional Subjective; (3) Rational Resisters are Resisters who are Rational Objective; (4) Traditionalists are Resisters who are Emotional Subjective.

A further discussion of change processes includes Lewin's concepts (See p. 62) of unfreezing, change, and refreezing; an expansion of these concepts as described by Schein ("Management Development as a Process of Influence." INDUSTRIAL MANAGEMENT REVIEW. School of Industrial Management, M.I.T., 1961, 2(11), 1-19.) and Greiner's findings (See above, this page) of factors differentiating successful from unsuccessful efforts.

The first part of this chapter concludes in caution: "The underlying dilemma exists for a behavioral scientist when he feels forced to identify himself either with the values of scientific inquiry or with the values of change advocacy."

Part two elaborates problems inherent in applying classical research designs to studies of organizational change, focusing on alternative designs "that could be worked out around environmental alternatives, subject involvement alterations, and experimenter involvement alterations."

Topics

Change Processes	Research Designs
Change Strategy	Resistance to Change
Refreezing	Support
	Unfreezing

Barrett, Jon H. INDIVIDUAL GOALS AND ORGANIZATIONAL OBJECTIVES: A STUDY OF INTEGRATING MECHANISMS. Ann Arbor: Center for Research on Utilization of Scientific Knowledge, University of Michigan, 1970. ix, 119 p.

This study was conducted with data collected from 1,781 employees of a refinery. The Institute for Social Research's Survey of Organizations questionnaire was used. Integration was examined with regard to the three mechanisms of accommodation, socialization, and exchange.

"The overall results . . . justify the conclusion that the degree of goal integration present is significantly related to the quality of an organization's functioning and the reactions of individuals to their membership in the organization.

"The three models differ in the strength of their relationship to goal integration, the accommodation model showing the strongest relationships, with the socialization model in second place and the exchange model showing low and sometimes negative relationships to goal integration.

"Rather than calling for either (a) the universal application of participative practices and universal rejection of classical methods or (b) the use, in a given situation of either participative or classical practices, our data suggest a third alternative, namely the universal application of participative management practices, supplemented in particular situations by the use of some practices called for by classical theories."

Topics

Accommodation	Participation
Goals (Individual/Organizational)	Socialization
	Survey of Organizations

Beer, Michael, and Huse, Edgar F. "A Systems Approach to Organization Development." JOURNAL OF APPLIED BEHAVIORAL SCIENCE 8, no. 1 (1972): 79-101.

An input-process-output model of organization is suggested as a useful basis for planned change efforts. Several strategies and technologies were used to change important dimensions included in the model. Generalizations are presented, including the following: OD efforts must not always start at the top; the organization itself is the best laboratory for learning; structural and interpersonal changes must complement one another; adult learning starts with behavior change rather than cognitive change; and the selection of change leaders as initial targets for the change program is a useful OD strategy.

Topics

Change Mechanisms	Influence
Change Phases	Job Enrichment
Change Strategy	Laboratory Approach
Change Technology	Learning
Commitment	Planned Change
Communications	System Model
Feedback	T-Group

Benne, Kenneth D., and Birnbaum, Max. "Principles of Changing." In THE PLANNING OF CHANGE, edited by Warren G. Bennis, Kenneth D. Benne, and Robert Chin, pp. 328-35. New York: Holt, Rinehart and Winston, 1969.

Lewin's model of change is presented, including an analysis of change in terms of the use of situational forces to accomplish unfreezing, moving, and refreezing. Three general change strategies are suggested based on increasing the driving forces, decreasing the restraining forces, and doing both these things.

Several strategies for achieving institutional change are suggested, centering on the following issues: environmental influences; system wide change; identification and evaluation of stress points; identification of beginning points; consideration of both informal and formal aspects of the organization; and participant involvement.

Topics

Change Processes   Informal Organization
Change Strategy   Situational Forces
Formal Organization   Stress

Bennis, Warren G. "A New Role for Behavioral Science: Effecting Organization Change." ADMINISTRATIVE SCIENCE QUARTERLY 8 (1963): 125-65.

Presents seven types of change programs. The first six are exposition and propagation, elite corps, psychoanalytic insight, staff, scholarly consultations, and circulation of ideas to the elite. The seventh type of change program is planned change. "Planned change can be defined as a deliberate and collaborative process involving a change-agent and client system," the author writes.

Bennis sets forth a framework for planned organizational change and relates each change model to "selected aspects of change induction." These include mechanisms for change, target of change, normative goals, functions of management, role of change agents, instrumentation of programs, and the means of change.

Topics

Change Agent   Change Strategy
Change Goals   Management
Change Processes   Planned Change

_____. "Theory and Method in Applying Behavioral Science to Planned Organizational Change." JOURNAL OF APPLIED BEHAVIORAL SCIENCE 1, no. 4 (1965): 337-60.

Bennis discusses the emergence of an action role for behavioral scientists. He focuses on the "planned change" approach (see above). "The process of planned change involves a change agent, a client system, and the collaborative attempt to apply valid knowledge to the client's problems."

This article is mostly an abbreviated version of Bennis's CHANGING ORGANIZATIONS (1966).

Topics

Change Agent   Planned Change
Change Strategy   Valid Information

Bowers, David G. "Perspectives in Organizational Development." Technical

Report to the Office of Naval Research, 1970. (Available from Defense Documentation Center, Cameron Station, Alexandria, Va.)

This theoretical statement of problems in organizational development
reviews those aspects of change practice with major theoretical implications, formulating a series of researchable questions. It also
discusses the potential relevance of certain aspects of clinical practice and learning theory to organizational development."

Topics

Attitude/Attitude Change	Learning
Authoritarianism	Organization Effectiveness
Behavior Change	Organization Goal/Task
Change Agent	Planned Change
Change Processes	Resistance to Change
Change Strategy	Sensitivity Training
Cognitive Change	T-Group
Consultation	Therapy
Diagnosis/Evaluation	

Bowers, David G.; Franklin, Jerome L.; and Pecorella, Patricia A. "Matching Problems, Precursors, and Interventions in OD: A Systemic Approach."
JOURNAL OF APPLIED BEHAVIORAL SCIENCE 11, no. 4 (1975): 391-409.

"A framework for systematic organizational development including
a model for matching interventions with problem causes is developed, using concepts from social systems theory and medical science
pathology. At the foundation of the framework are three basic
principles of change applicable both to physical and social systems.
These principles suggest that 1) interventions designed to change
leadership behavior must be selected to fit properties of the system,
2) certain areas or aspects of systems are predisposed to successful
change, and 3) change occurs indirectly through a series of cause/
effect successions.

"Potential interventions are classified in accordance with a scheme
identifying each intervention according to one of three basic problem causes or 'precursors.' The precursors include (a) level of information, (b) level of skill, and (c) aspects of situations in which
behavior occurs. Systematic organizational development is presented as a process of identifying and matching problem behavior,
precursors, and appropriate interventions. Implications for practitioners are presented, along with illustrations suggesting the advantages of this approach" (p. 391).

Topics

Change Strategy	Intervention
Diagnosis	Leadership

Bowers, David G., and Norman, Robert. "Strategies for Changing an Organization." INNOVATION 1 (1969): 50-55.

A plea is made for systematic organizational development efforts
which take into account the necessity of compatibility between social and technical components of systems. "A program of planned
organizational change should avoid two mistakes. The first is changing one condition exclusively for all, or even for most groups.
Second, the program should not ignore or deny the relevance of
the system and its functioning in favor of producing 'better
people.'"

Solid information about the system to be changed as well as other
systems is viewed as a necessary basis for change. "Any change
treatment should be based upon solid information about how other
more effective organizations function; second, research should be
done into the nature of the organization to be changed." The
authors emphasize the need for "measurement that is precise, accurate, conceptually sound and relevant."

The diagnostic and therapeutic processes of a change effort are
conceived as separate but related.

Topics

Diagnosis/Evaluation   Sociotechnical Systems
Measurement   Therapy

Burke, W. Warner. "A Comparison of Management Development and Organization Development." JOURNAL OF APPLIED BEHAVIORAL SCIENCE 7, no.
5 (1971): 569-79.

In an effort to clarify the conceptualization and practice of organization and management development, they are compared on six
dimensions: reasons for use, goals, typical interventions, time
frame, staff requirements, and values. (See also Burke and
Schmidt, p. 29).

Topics

Change Strategy   Management Training/
Intervention   Development
                                        Values

_____. "The Demise of Organization Development." JOURNAL OF CON-
TEMPORARY BUSINESS 1, no. 3 (1972): 57-63.

Burke raises the question of whether current activities called organization development are actually planned efforts to change an organization's culture or are merely adaptations to changes that occur in the organization's environment.

"What then is OD? It is a planned, sustained effort to change
an organization's culture. From what type of culture to what other
kind? From a closed culture, characterized by decision-making
vested in authority of position; inflexibility or organizational structure; and one reward system . . . to a culture of openness; deci-

sion-making as a function of authority of expertise, competence, and information; flexible organizational structures adaptive to changing needs and functions; and a variable reward system, in which employees have choices."

According to Burke, OD practitioners are overly "involved with bits and pieces of OD technology," helping organizations to adapt but not facilitating systematic efforts at planned change. He suggests that more emphasis is needed on power confrontation.

Topics

Adaptation   Culture
Change Technology   Power

_____. "Organization Development in Transition." JOURNAL OF APPLIED BEHAVIORAL SCIENCE 12, no. 1 (1976): 22-43.

This article addresses itself to the evolution of organization development over the past twelve years, an evolution that the authors consider to be adaptive rather than planned and deliberate. These changes represent value shifts, expanded technology and theory, modifications in OD strategy, and a growing legitimization of OD as a field. Three recommendations are made for the future survival of OD: (1) OD must become more theoretical and research-based; (2) OD must develop a new model that will combine its methodology with directions for organization change based on research knowledge; and (3) OD needs practitioners who are self-assured and dedicated to implementing OD.

Topics

Change Agent   Consultation
Change Strategy   Diagnosis/Evaluation
Change Technology   Values

Burke, W. Warner, and Schmidt, Warren H. "Primary Target for Change: The Manager or the Organization?" In ORGANIZATIONAL FRONTIERS AND HUMAN VALUES, edited by W.H. Schmidt, pp. 151-74. Belmont, Calif.: Wadsworth, 1970.

The authors present a comparison of two basic approaches to the improvement of managerial effectiveness within an organization: (a) management development--the educational development of individual managers; and (b) organization development (OD)--the development of the organizational units of people.

Issues emphasized include the integration of the individual and organization, the range of interventions used in development efforts, the team as a basic organizational unit, the necessity of a supportive climate, and competencies required in a development staff (see also Burke, "A Comparison of Management Development and Organization Development," above).

Topics

Action Research
Change Agent
Climate
Individual-Organization
Interface

Management Training/
Development
Survey Feedback
Team Building/Development

Chin, Robert. "The Utility System Models and Developmental Models for Practitioners." In THE PLANNING OF CHANGE, edited by Warren G. Bennis, Kenneth D. Benne, and Robert Chin, pp. 297-312. New York: Holt, Rinehart and Winston, 1969.

Chin presents concepts necessary to understanding the use of a 'system' model and a 'developmental' model for human events. The benefits of these models are also outlined. The system model includes the following elements: boundary, tension, stress, strain and conflict, equilibrium and "steady state," and feedback. "By developmental models, we mean those bodies of thought that center around growth and directional change." Chin discusses several assumptions of such models.

Topics

Change Models
Change Processes
Conflict/Conflict Resolution

Developmental Model
System Model
System Theory

Chin, Robert, and Benne, Kenneth D. "General Strategies for Effecting Changes in Human Systems." In THE PLANNING OF CHANGE, edited by Warren G. Bennis, Kenneth D. Benne, and Robert Chin, pp. 32-59. New York: Holt, Rinehart and Winston, 1969.

The authors illustrate three strategies of deliberate change in terms of historical development with regard to approaches to change and the persons associated with each strategy. The strategies are termed: rational-empirical, normative-reeducative, and power-coercive.

In focusing upon the normative-reeducative strategy, the authors examine the range of change-agent interventions and the elements common to various aspects in this approach.

Topics

Change Agent
Change Strategy
Feedback

Planned Change
Problem Solving
Sociotechnical Systems

Clark, James V. "A Healthy Organization." In THE PLANNING OF CHANGE, edited by Warren G. Bennis, Kenneth D. Benne, and Robert Chin, pp. 282-97. New York: Holt, Rinehart and Winston, 1969.

"I consider an organization to be healthy if its members observe certain unstated but quite uniform codes of behavior which they accept as normal things to do, provided these codes produce behavior which allows all levels of the organization to meet two basic but diverse requirements--maintenance of the status quo, and growth.

"On balance and over time the healthy organization is one in which its component parts--group and individual--somehow manage to achieve an optimal resolution of their tendencies toward equilibrium (maintenance, homeostasis, status quo or call it what you will) and their capacities for growth (elaboration, complication, differentiation, negative entropy, or what not).

"Any organization which was set up only to meet the needs of individuals to grow, or to participate, or to be creative, or what not, and which did not consider the needs of people to form into groups, or of the total organization to engage in satisfactory transactions with outside groups such as stockholders or customers, cannot be considered healthy."

Clark notes that neither humanism nor efficiency can be achieved if either is valued to the exclusion of the other.

Topics

Goals (Individual/Organization)   Organization Growth
Group Processes   Organization Health
Organization Effectiveness   Values

Dalton, Gene W. "Influence and Organizational Change." In ORGANIZATIONAL CHANGE AND DEVELOPMENT, edited by Gene W. Dalton, Paul R. Lawrence, and Larry E. Greiner, pp. 230-58. Homewood, Ill.: Irwin-Dorsey, 1970.

A model of the influence process in organizational change is presented and elaborated. The model is based on progressions through the following stages: tension experienced within the system; intervention of a prestigious influencing agent; individuals attempt to implement the proposed changes; new behavior and attitudes reinforced by achievement, social ties, and internalized values--accompanied by decreasing dependence on influencing agent.

Topics

Change Phases   Influence
Change Processes

Davis, Sheldon A. "An Organic Problem-Solving Method of Organizational Change." JOURNAL OF APPLIED BEHAVIORAL SCIENCE 3, no. 1 (1967): 3-21.

An argument is presented against a "soft" interpretation of McGregor's ideas in the context of describing organizational development activities and general philosophies at TRW Systems.

An emphasis on confrontation is credited with helping to improve relationships among interdependent individuals and groups. "There is not real growth, there is no real development in the organization or in the individuals within it, if they do not confront and deal directly with their problems. They can get together and share feelings, but if that's all they do, it's merely a catharsis." The use of task-related laboratories is seen as useful. Laboratories involving three major elements are described: (1) preparation including orientation to the theory and rationale behind laboratories, questions, and responses from trainers, and questions for participants to think about; (2) a three- or four-day laboratory; (3) three or four one-night sessions to discuss carryover of the laboratory experience to the job.

Topics

Confrontation
Laboratory Training

Problem Solving
Team Building/Development

Elden, James M.; Goldstone, Raymond; and Brown, Michael K. "The University as an Organizational Frontier." In ORGANIZATIONAL FRONTIERS AND HUMAN VALUES, edited by Warren H. Schmidt, pp. 87-101. Belmont, Calif.: Wadsworth, 1970.

Universities are presented as a model of knowledge-based organizations which are to become more significant in the future. "As society moves into the post-industrial era, knowledge-based organizations become increasingly significant. Post-industrial society is above all a knowledge-dependent society. Its organizations are dependent on high levels of technical and professional expertise and information-handling capacities. As organizations function more on a knowledge base, they begin to function more like university organizations with shared power, highly mobile members, and non-operational goals."

Four major themes are discussed in terms of challenges for future organizational development efforts: confronting the politics of change; developing interorganizational linkages; coping with rapid change; and expanding organizational development perspectives.

Topics

Expertise·
Knowledge-Based Organization

Linkage
Politics of Change
University

Fink, Stephen L.; Beak, Joel; and Taddeo, Kenneth. "Organizational Crisis and Change." JOURNAL OF APPLIED BEHAVIORAL SCIENCE 7, no. 1 (1971): 15-37.

A four-stage model is presented for dealing with organizational crisis and change, with application for the individual extrapolated to organizational parameters. The four stages are: shock, defensive retreat, acknowledgment, and adaptation and change.

The phases are described in terms of interpersonal relations, inter-group relations, communication, leadership and decision making, problem handling, planning and goal setting, and structure.

Topics

Communications	Intergroup Processes
Crisis	Leadership
Decision Making	Problem Solving
Group Development	Structure

French, Wendell L., and Bell, Cecil H., Jr., ORGANIZATION DEVELOP-MENT: BEHAVIORAL SCIENCE INTERVENTIONS FOR ORGANIZATION IM-PROVEMENT. Englewood Cliffs, N.J.: Prentice-Hall, 1973.

"Organization development is the name given to the emerging ap-plied behavioral science discipline that seeks to improve organiza-tions through planned, systematic, long-range efforts focused on the organizations culture and its human and social processes" (p. xiv). "In this book we present what we think is the field of or-ganization development: we show where it came from and where it may be going, and we give the reader a look at both the the-ory and practice of OD." Included are materials "that we hope will make the work relevant to academicians, to students, . . . to OD specialists, and to practicing managers who may want to try to improve their organizations" (p. xv).

Contents

1. Some Illustrations of Organization Development Efforts
2. A Definition of Organization Development
3. A History of Organization Development
4. Operational Components
5. Characteristics and Foundations of the OD Process
6. Underlying Assumptions and Values
7. Relevant Systems Concepts
8. Action Research and Organization Development
9. OD Interventions--An Overview
10. Team Interventions
11. Intergroup Interventions
12. Total Organizational Interventions
13. Personal, Interpersonal, and Group Process Interventions
14. Conditions for Optimal Success
15. System Ramifications and New Demands
16. Issues in Consultant-Client Relationships
17. Mechanistic and Organic Systems
18. The Future of OD

Topics

Action Research	Change Strategy
Change Agent	Change Technology

Consultant	Mechanistic Systems
Diagnosis/Evaluation	Organic Systems
Feedback	Process Consultation
Grid Organizational Development	Role
Intergroup Process	Sensitivity Training
Job Design	Survey Feedback
Job Enrichment	Team Building/Development
Laboratory Training	T-Group
Leadership	Third-Party Intervention
Management by Objectives	Values
Managerial Grid	

Friedlander, Frank. "OD Reaches Adolescence: An Exploration of its Under-lying Values." JOURNAL OF APPLIED BEHAVIORAL SCIENCE 12, no. 1 (1976): 7-21.

According to Friedlander three philosophies or sets of values--ra-tionalism, pragmatism, existentialism--serve as the basis for describ-ing the development and current state of the field of organizational development. "Rationalism pushes contemporary OD toward becom-ing more scientific, more theoretical and conceptual, more logical, more mathematical; toward abstract models; toward building theories; toward understanding the determinants of our organizational, social and personal worlds. Pragmatism pushes OD in the direction of be-coming more useful--how does OD increase effectiveness, perfor-mance, productivity; how can OD determine expected or alternative organizational processes and structures, and how can it feed back information into the organization to reduce the gap between the way it is now and the way it would be better? Existentialism within OD pushes the organization to become more humanistic, more aware, more emerging, more person-growth oriented."

Topics

Values

Golembiewski, Robert T., and Muzenrider, Robert. "Social Desirability as an Intervening Variable in Interpreting OD Effects." JOURNAL OF APPLIED BEHAVIORAL SCIENCE 11, no. 3 (1975): 317-32.

This study explores the usefulness of taking "social desirability" (SD) differences into account in interpreting any effects of OD interventions measured by self-reports. Results indicate "SD dif-ferences can mask measurements of such effects, especially in be-fore versus after designs" (p. 317).

Topics

Crowne-Marlowe Social	Social Desirability
Desirability Scale	
Likert Profile	

Greiner, Larry E. "Antecedents of Planned Organizational Change." JOUR-

NAL OF APPLIED BEHAVIORAL SCIENCE 3, no. 1 (1967): 51-86.

This article charts the history of an organization and its management prior to a decision to begin a Managerial Grid organization development program. The company in question had been in a very stable environment and, upon finding itself in a new environment, had encountered problems in adapting.

Greiner identifies two stages preceding the initiation of the change activities: arousal-and-search and recognition-and-decision. During the first stage, "members of that organization will (a) perceive the new demands as threatening and feel resentful and unable to cope with these demands, and (b) they will behave defensively to resist the new demands while searching for a way out of their dilemma, so long as the environment continues to press its original demands upon the organization." During the second stage, "members of that top group will (a) perceive that they indeed have serious organization problems and feel a desire to solve these problems, and (b) they will behave by seeking advice from the expert and will decide to attempt a major organizational change, so long as the environment relieves pressure and the outside expert furnishes a program of action."

Topics

Adaptation	Environment
Antecedents to Change	Managerial Grid
Change Processes	Resistance to Change

Greiner, Larry E., and Barnes, Louis B. "Organizational Change and Development." In ORGANIZATIONAL CHANGE AND DEVELOPMENT, edited by Gene W. Dalton, Paul R. Lawrence, and Larry E. Greiner, pp. 1-12. Homewood, Ill.: Irwin-Dorsey, 1970.

This chapter serves as an introduction to a volume edited by Dalton, Lawrence, and Greiner (See p. 51).

The two overarching objectives of organizational change as described in this chapter are "(1) changes in an organization's level of adaptation to its environment, and (2) changes in the internal behavioral patterns of employees."

Seen as cutting across all approaches to organizational change are four common demoninators: plan (from structured to unstructured), power (from unilateral to delegated), relationships (from impersonal to personal), and tempo (from revolutionary to evolutionary).

The authors delineate four areas of decision making for the involved manager: diagnosing problems, planning for change, launching the change, and following up to assess what has happened.

Topics

Adaptation	Change Processes
Behavior Patterns	Diagnosis/Evaluation

Harrison, Roger. "Choosing the Depth of Organizational Intervention." JOUR-
NAL OF APPLIED BEHAVIORAL SCIENCE 6, no. 2 (1970): 181-202.

The depth of emotional involvement in change processes is used
as a basis for differentiating among change strategies. "By depth
we mean how deep, value-laden, emotionally charged, and central
to the individuals' sense of self are the issues and processes about
which a consultant attempts directly to obtain information and
which he seeks to influence" (p. 181).

The consequences of intervening at different depths are discussed
and two criteria are suggested "for choosing the appropriate depth
of intervention: first, to intervene at a level no deeper than that
required to produce enduring solutions to the problems at hand;
and second, to intervene at a level no deeper than that at which
the energy and resources of the client can be committed to problem solving and to change" (p. 201).

Topics

Autonomy	Intervention
Change Agent	Laboratory Approach
Change Strategy	Management by Objectives
Commitment	Managerial Grid
Confrontation	Norms
Consultant	Operations Analysis
Consultation	Resistance to Change
Dependency	Sensitivity Training
Diagnosis/Evaluation	Task Group Therapy
Ethics	T-Group
Goals (Individual/	Values
Organizational)	

Hornstein, Harvey A.; Bunker, Barbara B.; and Hornstein, M.G. "Some Conceptual Issues in Individual and Group-Oriented Strategies of Intervention into
Organizations." JOURNAL OF APPLIED BEHAVIORAL SCIENCE 7, no. 5
(1971): 557-67.

Assumptions underlying individual and group-oriented strategies of
intervention are explored. Individual change is described in terms
of four approaches: (1) analytic--the processes underlying individual
behavior also underlie organizational behavior, (2) behaviorist--be-
havior and not internal processes should be the focus of change,
(3) social-psychological--social norms are the major determinants
of individual behavior, and (4) Socratic-rational--change results
from knowledge and understanding. The individual strategies are
the focus of three concerns described by the authors as: difficulties in transferring learnings from learning settings to work situations, a "critical mass" of changed individuals needed to change
a system, and resistance to individual change because of pressures
created by social norms.

Organizational development is described as the most prominent of the change techniques aimed at group-level phenomena. According to the authors, three steps precede OD "to make the organization safe for use of [the] techniques:" (1) "entry aims at creating a felt need for change," (2) "normative change . . . is aimed at exposing increasingly large numbers of organization members to the new social norms," and (3)"structural change . . . involves the placement of OD advocates in positions that provide them with the flexibility, prestige, and protection necessary to conduct further OD projects."

Topics

Change Strategies   Resistance to Change
Entry   Structural Change
Group Change   Transfer of Training
Individual Change

House, Robert J. "Management Development is a Game." HARVARD BUSINESS REVIEW 41, no. 4 (1963): 130-43.

The author suggests that many efforts at management development have failed to improve operational results because of a lack of understanding regarding the nature of the needed changes, unwillingness of change on the part of supervisors, and an environment that is resistant to change.

Measurement techniques are suggested as a way "to identify development needs, to predict results, and to choose the proper methods."

Topics

Management Training/   Measurement
Development   Resistance to Change

Huse, Edgar F., and Beer, Michael. "Eclectic Approach to Organizational Development." HARVARD BUSINESS REVIEW 49, no. 5 (1971): 103-12.

Organizational development activities in four departments of a plant are used to illustrate an approach emphasizing the application of interventions to coincide with the preferences of managers. In each case the OD approach was "dictated not by economics or technology but by the manager's personal choice." Changes in several criteria measures (e.g., productivity, rejects, absenteeism, quality) are offered as evidence of the general success of this eclectic approach to OD.

Topics

Change Agents   Group Processes
Change Strategy   Job Enrichment
Communications   Leadership
Diagnosis

Jenks, R. Stephen. "An Action-Research Approach to Organizational Change."
JOURNAL OF APPLIED BEHAVIORAL SCIENCE 6, no. 2 (1970): 131-48.

The development and usage of an organizational Q-sort instrument
is described and evaluated in terms of (a) the usefulness of the
instrument, (b) the extent to which it is a meaningful part of an
organizational change and development project, and (c) the results obtained.

Topics

| Action Research | Feedback |
| Diagnosis/Evaluation | Q-Sort |

Kahn, Robert L. "Organizational Development: Some Problems and Proposals."
JOURNAL OF APPLIED BEHAVIORAL SCIENCE 10, no. 4 (1974): 485-502.

The stated purpose of the author is to "cite some problems, the
resolution of which will facilitate" the transition of organizational
development "from being a miscellany of uncertain devices to be-
coming a mature, usable set of principles and procedures for organizational change."

Among the major problems identified are (1) the lack of support
for accepted theoretical propositions; (e.g., Lewin's ideas of unfreezing change, and freezing; the necessity for "starting at the
top"; the value of participation of those involved in the change);
(2) the lack of specificity in defining the events and behaviors
behind common labels used in the OD literature and (3) the emphasis on autobiographical accounts and lack of attention given
the total organization as the ultimate target of change activities.

"The penultimate problem that I wish to raise about organizational
development is the separation of structure and process," Kahn
writes. This separation is seen as misleading since structure consists of patterns of behaviors and "To change an organization means
changing the patterns of recurring behavior, and that is by definition a change in organizational structure." A distinction is drawn
between role prescriptions (e.g., formal expectations) and role elaborations (e.g., actual role behaviors). The author suggests that
changes in structure refer to the former, while changes in process
refer to role elaborations.

Topics

Change Processes	Role Elaboration
Job Design	Role Prescription
Process	Structural Change
Research Designs	Structure
Role	

Katz, Daniel, and Kahn, Robert [L]. "Organizational Change." In their THE
SOCIAL PSYCHOLOGY OF ORGANIZATIONS, pp. 390-451. New York:
John Wiley & Sons, 1966.

This chapter includes a useful conceptual framework for understanding approaches to organizational change, as well as an excellent summary of some important studies in the area.

Seven approaches to organizational change are suggested together with examples. The approaches include information, individual counseling and therapy, influence of the peer group, sensitivity training, group therapy, feedback, and systemic change. Systemic change is considered the most powerful approach by these authors.

Topics

Change Strategy   Sensitivity Training
Counseling   Systemic Change
Feedback   Therapy
Influence

Katzell, Raymond A., Yankelovich, Daniel, et al. "Improving Productivity and Job Satisfaction." ORGANIZATIONAL DYNAMICS 4 (Summer 1975): 69-77.

The central discussion of this review article addresses the question of how economic performance and worker satisfaction can be increased together. After arguing that these two goals are not necessarily related, the authors suggest that motivation is the key to attaining increases in both performance and satisfaction.

Six critical ingredients provide a summary statement of what characterizes organizations which meet these dual goals. Also, an eight-question checklist is offered to evaluate a particular organization's structure.

Topics

Commitment   Motivation
Control   Performance
Job Design   Reward System
Job Enlargement   Satisfaction

King, Albert S. "Expectation Effects in Organizational Change." ADMINISTRATIVE SCIENCE QUARTERLY 19 (1974): 221-30.

A two-by-two experimental design is employed in four clothing pattern design plants to evaluate the differential effects of two forms of job enrichment (job enlargement, job rotation) and two sets of management expectations (increased output, no change in output but improved industrial relations). Analyses indicate that the expectations of managers are more important sources of variation in results than are the innovations themselves.

Topics

Absenteeism   Job Design
Attitude/Attitude Change   Job Enlargement
Change Processes   Job Enrichment
Expectations   Job Rotation

39

Lawrence, Paul R. "How to Deal with Resistance to Change." HARVARD BUSINESS REVIEW 47, no. 1 (1969): 4-12, 166.

This is a reprint of an earlier article with added comments by the author.

Change, according to Lawrence, has both technical and social aspects. "The technical aspect of the change is the making of a measurable modification in the physical routines of the job. The social aspect of the change refers to the way those affected by it think it will alter their established relationships in the organization."

This author argues that it is the social aspect that affects resistance to change more than the technical aspect. Two studies are cited as support for this idea.

Topics

Resistance to Change　　　　　　　Technological Change
Social Change

Lippitt, Gordon L., and Schmidt, Warren H. "Crises in a Developing Organization." HARVARD BUSINESS REVIEW 45, no. 6 (1967): 102-12.

Six critical stages in the life of organizations are proposed: creation, survival, stability, pride and reputation, uniqueness and adaptability, and contribution. According to these authors, it is during the fifth stage that organizational development efforts take place.

Topics

Change Processes　　　　　　　Organization Life
Organization Development

Morse, Nancy [C.], and Reimer, Everett. "The Experimental Change of a Major Organizational Variable." JOURNAL OF ABNORMAL AND SOCIAL PSYCHOLOGY 52 (1956); 120-29.

The authors describe a field experiment in which an attempt was made to change satisfaction and productivity by changing the level of decision-making processes in a clerical organization.

As expected, individual satisfaction was increased with a lowering of the decision-making process and was decreased with a decrease in local decision making. Contrary to expectation, costs declined more in the program which raised the level of decision making than in those areas where the decision-making process was lowered.

Topics

Decision Making　　　　　　　Satisfaction
Productivity

Mouton, Jane S., and Blake, Robert R. "Behavioral Science Theories Underlying Organization Development." JOURNAL OF CONTEMPORARY BUSINESS 1, no. 3 (1972): 9-22.

The Managerial Grid is used as a framework for comparing a variety of theories which have contributed to the field of organization development. Contributions are noted in a variety of areas by different individuals. Noted for their emphasis on production are Weber, Fayol, and Taylor. An emphasis on people is attributed to Mayo, Roethlisberger and Dickson, Barnard, and Lewin. Those emphasizing production through people include Trist and Bamforth, Herzberg, Likert, McGregor, Argyris, and Etzioni. The roots of organization development as it is known today are attributed to work done at Esso Standard Oil Company in 1956 by Blake, Shepard, and Mouton.

The following conditions are suggested as necessary for systematic development: involvement of the whole organization; leadership from those who head the organization; initiation and guidance from within the organization; the employment of systematic ways of thinking and analysis; and an effort which proceeds in a sequential, orderly way.

Topics

Change Strategy   Managerial Grid

Nord, Walter R. "The Failure of Current Applied Behavioral Science--A Marxian Perspective." JOURNAL OF APPLIED BEHAVIORAL SCIENCE 10, no. 4 (1974): 557-78.

A comparison is drawn between the values of applied behavioral scientists and the work of Marx to examine the potential benefits of considering socioeconomic variables in efforts aimed at changing managerial practices. Among the key areas explored are the design of work, alienation, change, and the role of science in human development.

Topics

Alienation   Socioeconomic
Management   Values
Marx

NTL Institute for Applied Behavioral Science. "What is OD?" In SENSITIVITY TRAINING AND THE LABORATORY APPROACH, edited by Robert T. Golembiewski and Arthur Blumberg, pp. 342-45. Itasca, Ill.: F.E. Peacock, 1970.

Descriptions are presented of the behavioral science findings and hypotheses underlying OD, the objectives of OD, and technology associated with OD.

Topics

Change Strategy   Individual-Organization
Goals (Individual/Organizational) Interface

Pelz, Donald C. "Influence: A Key to Effective Leadership in the First-Line Supervisor." PERSONNEL 29, no. 3 (1952): 209-17.

> The results of a study conducted at Detroit Edison Company indicate that influence is a key variable in determining the effect that leadership behaviors will have on subordinates.
>
> "The supervisory behaviors of 'siding with employees' and 'social closeness to employees' will tend to raise employee satisfaction only if the supervisor has enough influence to make these behaviors pay off in terms of actual benefits for employees," the author concludes.

Topics

Influence   Satisfaction
Leadership

Sashkin, Marshall; Morris, William C.; and Horst, Leslie. "A Comparison of Social and Organizational Change Models: Information Flow and Data Use Processes." PSYCHOLOGICAL REVIEW 80, no. 6 (1973): 510-26.

> Change-agent roles (consultant, trainer, researcher) serve as the basis for examining five models of social and organizational change. The models include those termed: (1) research, development, and diffusion; (2) social interaction and diffusion; (3) intervention theory and method; (4) planned change; and (5) action research. On the basis of a comparison across the five models, the authors conclude that the action-research model is the best for effective attainment of adaptive change in social systems.

Topics

Action Research   Change Technology
Change Agent   Consultant
Change Strategy   Intervention
                                       Process

Schein, Edgar H. "The Mechanisms of Change." In THE PLANNING OF CHANGE, edited by Warren G. Bennis, Kenneth D. Benne, and Robert Chin, pp. 98-107. New York: Holt, Rinehart and Winston, 1969.

> Schein presents a theoretical discussion of change based on Lewin's model which includes the stages of unfreezing, changing, and refreezing. He suggests mechanisms for implementing each stage in the change process. Unfreezing may come about through lack of confirmation or disconfirmation, induction of guilt-anxiety, and/or creation of psychological safety by reduction of threat or removal of barriers. Changing occurs through the mechanism of cognitive redefinition (either identification or Scanning). Refreezing occurs through integrating new responses into personality or integrating new response into significant ongoing relationships through reconfirmation.
>
> An analysis of two types of identification (defensive and positive)

is also presented. The analysis focuses on conditions for the processes, psychological processes involved, and outcomes.

Topics

Change Phases	Identification
Change Processes	Refreezing
Changing	Unfreezing

Shepard, Herbert A. "Changing Interpersonal and Intergroup Relationships in Organizations." In HANDBOOK OF ORGANIZATIONS, edited by James G. March, pp. 1115-43. Chicago: Rand-McNally, 1965.

Shepard describes the assumptions and dimensions of the concepts of "primary" and "secondary mentalities" and the relationship between these concepts and organizational effectiveness.

Several aspects of interpersonal and intergroup relations are discussed with reference to ways of improving them. Various forms of laboratory training are suggested as techniques for changing these relationships. "The most powerful educative experience presently known for inducing rapid movement from internalized primary assumptions to internalized secondary assumptions is the so-called laboratory method of training--in particular the T-group," the author notes.

"The main point of this chapter is that a more humanistic organization theory than we have known in the past is required, and that it is realizable in practice."

Topics

Change Agent	Management
Collaboration	Primary Mentality
Conflict/Conflict Resolution	Problem Solving
Diagnosis/Evaluation	Risk/Risk-Taking
Family Laboratory	Secondary Mentality
Group Processes	Stranger Laboratory
Intergroup Processes	T-Group
Interpersonal Processes	Work Group
Laboratory Training	

Simmonds, Geoffrey R. "Organization Development: A Key to Future Growth." PERSONNEL ADMINISTRATION 30, no. 1 (1967): 19-24.

A company president describes experiences encountered when his organization used the Managerial Grid and T-groups in a development program. A favorable picture is presented, emphasizing the "latent mental resources" that are available but seldom used in industry.

Topics

Human Resources	T-Group
Managerial Grid	

Starbuck, William H. "Organizational Growth and Development." In HAND-
BOOK OF ORGANIZATIONS, edited by James G. March, pp. 451-533.
Chicago: Rand-McNally, 1965.

Studies which emphasize organizational growth and development
are reviewed. "Growth is defined as change in an organization's
size when size is measured by the organization's membership or
employment; development is defined as change in an organization's
age."

The major sections of this chapter explore motives for growth,
adaptation and growth, models of growth, and administrative structure and growth.

Three types of change are distinguished: ultimate goals, task structure, and social structure.

Topics

Adaptation	Organization Development
Administrative Structure	Organization Growth
Cost	Power
Environment	Prestige
Flexibility	Profit
Goals (Individual/Organizational)	Risk/Risk-Taking
Management	Security
Motivation	Self-Realization
Organization Age	Stability
	Survival

Tagliere, Daniel A. "What an Executive Should Know about Organization
Development." TRAINING AND DEVELOPMENT JOURNAL 29 (July 1975):
34-40.

Within a very broad definition--i.e., "any planned effort directed
toward helping the members of an organization to interact more
effectively in pursuit of the organization's goals"--descriptions are
provided of several OD strategies, including management by objectives, team building, job enrichment/enlargement, sociotechnical redesign, force field analysis, conflict resolution, intergroup
merging, future shock absorbing, feedback, team development,
multiple management, and training.

Topics

Change Strategy	Job Design
Change Technology	Job Enlargement
Conflict/Conflict Resolution	Job Enrichment
Feedback	Management by Objectives
Force Field Analysis	Multiple Management
Intergroup Merger	Team Building/Development

Tannenbaum, Robert. "Organizational Change Has to Come through Individual
Change." INNOVATION 23 (1971): 36-43.

The importance of interpersonal competence (social sensitivity and behavioral flexibility) is emphasized as the basis for organizational improvement.

Topics

Change Agent
Individual Change

Individual Growth
Interpersonal Competence

Watson, Goodwin. "Resistance to Change." In THE PLANNING OF CHANGE, edited by Warren G. Bennis, Kenneth D. Benne, and Robert Chin, pp. 488-98. New York: Holt, Rinehart and Winston, 1969.

Watson cites forces in personality and social systems provoking resistance to change. Resistance in personality results from homeostasis, habit, primacy, selective perception and retention, dependence, superego, self-distrust, insecurity, and regression. Forces causing resistance to change in social systems include conformity to norms, systematic and cultural coherence, vested interests, the sacrosanct, and rejection of outsiders.

Change situations in which resistance will be low and means for reducing resistance where it exists are discussed.

Topics

Resistance to Change

Weisbord, Marvin R. "The Gap between OD Practice and Theory--and Publication." JOURNAL OF APPLIED BEHAVIORAL SCIENCE 10, no. 4 (1974): 476-84.

This short article serves as a preface to a special issue of the JOURNAL OF APPLIED BEHAVIORAL SCIENCE devoted to OD practice and theory. The author reflects upon the articles included in this issue, stressing the theme that practice has advanced well beyond what is generally reflected in the literature. What is missing, according to this author, "are the structures and procedures for testing the ways clients and consultants translate theories into practice" (p. 484). (See also Kahn, p. 38; Golembiewski, Hilles, and Kagno, p. 89; Brown, Aram, and Bachner, p. 138; and Nord, p. 41).

Topics

Action Research
Consultant
Flex-Time

Intervention
Team Building

Zand, Dale E., and Sorensen, Richard E. "Theory of Change and the Effective Use of Management Science." ADMINISTRATIVE SCIENCE QUARTERLY 20, no. 4 (1975): 532-45.

This study of successful and unsuccessful application was based on

mail responses from 154 management scientists. An operationaliza-
tion of Lewin's ideas of unfreezing, moving, and refreezing (See
Lewin, p. 62) served as the basis for this investigation. Results
support the Lewin's theory indicating that "level of success, at
least from reports of management scientists on their change efforts,
was positively correlated with favorable forces and negatively correlated with unfavorable forces in each phase of change" (p. 541).

Topics

Change Phases	Resistance to Change
Change Processes	Unfreezing
Freezing	

Readings and Collected Case Studies

Bartlett, Alton C., and Kayser, Thomas A., eds. CHANGING ORGANIZA-
TIONAL BEHAVIOR. Englewood Cliffs, N.J.: Prentice Hall, 1973. xiii,
434 p.

This collection of readings includes several of the most frequently
cited authors and references in the field of organization development, together with short section introductions prepared by the
editors.

Contents

Part I: Organizational Change: Elements, Processes, and Perspectives
Organizational Change: A Trial Synthesis, Alton C.
Bartlett and Thomas A. Kayser
The Environment, Bureaucracy, and Social Change: A
Political Prognosis, Louis C. Gawthrop
Applied Organization Change in Industry: Structural,
Technical, and Human Approaches, Harold J. Leavitt
Patterns of Organization Change, Larry E. Greiner
Theory and Method in Applying Behavioral Science to
Planned Organizational Change, Warren G. Bennis
The Change Process in Organizations: An Applied Ap-
proach, Leonard R. Sayles
Part II: Feedback and Influence: Seeds for a Theory of Changing
Studying and Creating Change: A Means to Understand-
ing Social Organization, Floyd C. Mann
Changing Behavior through Simulation: An Alternate
Design to T-Group Training, Alton C. Bartlett
Management Development as a Process of Influence,
Edgar H. Schein
Influence and Organizational Change, Gene W. Dalton
Toward a Theory of Changing Behavior: An Elabora-
tion on the Role of Influence and Coercion, Alton
C. Bartlett and Thomas A. Kayser
Part III: Change Strategies in Action: Methods and Results
Laboratory Training and Organization Development, Paul
C. Buchanan

An Organic Problem-Solving Method of Organizational
Change, Sheldon A. Davis
Changing Behavior as a Means to Increased Efficiency,
Alton C. Bartlett
Breakthrough in Organization Development, Robert R.
Blake, Jane S. Mouton, Louis B. Barnes, and Larry
E. Greiner
The Design of Jobs, Louis E. Davis
Work Flow as the Basis for Organization Design, Eliot
D. Chapple and Leonard R. Sayles
Improving Patient Care through Organizational Changes
in the Mental Hospital, Elaine Cumming, I.L.W.
Clancey, and John Cumming
The Experimental Change of a Major Organizational
Variable, Nancy C. Morse and Everett Reimer
Part IV: Resistance to Change: Coping with a Critical Problem
The Problem of Resistance to Change in Industry, Robert
N. McMurry
How to Deal with Resistance to Change, Paul R. Lawr-
ence
Resistance to Change--Its Analysis and Prevention, Al-
vin Zander
Overcoming Resistance to Stability: A Time to Move;
A Time to Pause, Robert Albanese
Some Notes on the Dynamics of Resistance to Change:
The Defender Role, Donald Klein

Contributing Authors

Albanese, Robert
Barnes, Louis B.
Bartlett, Alton C.
Bennis, Warren G.
Blake, Robert R.
Buchanan, Paul C.
Chapple, Eliot D.
Clancey, I.L.W.
Cumming, Elaine
Cumming, John
Dalton, Gene W.
Davis, Louis E.
Davis, Sheldon A.
Gawthrop, Louis C.

Greiner, Larry E.
Kayser, Thomas A.
Klein, Donald
Lawrence, Paul R.
Leavitt, Harold J.
McMurry, Robert N.
Mann, Floyd C.
Morse, Nancy C.
Mouton, Jane S.
Reimer, Everett
Sayles, Leonard R.
Schein, Edgar H.
Zander, Alvin

Topics

Action Research
Behavior Change
Change Agent
Change Strategy
Feedback
Job Design

Laboratory Training
Managerial Grid
Participation
Research Designs
Resistance to Change
T-Group

Bennis, Warren G.; Benne, Kenneth D.; and Chin, Robert, eds. THE PLAN-
NING OF CHANGE. New York: Holt, Rinehart and Winston, 1969. 627 p.

This is the second edition of a large collection of readings on
planned change. Each chapter contains from three to eight se-
lections relevant to some aspect of this area. An introduction to
each chapter is provided by the editors.

Contents

Part One: The Evolution of Planned Change
   1. The roots of planned change
   2. Current and emergent notions about planned change
Part Two: Elements of Planned Change
   3. The utilization of scientific knowledge
   4. Collaboration and conflict
   5. Related theories of change and influence
   6. Systems in change
Part Three: Dynamics of Planned Change
   7. Change strategies
   8. Instrumentation
   9. Resistance
Part Four: Values and Goals
   10. Finding direction in planned change
   11. Some value dilemmas of the change agent

Contributing Authors

Argyris, C.	Gouldner, A.W.	McClelland, D.C.
Barnes, L.B.	Harrison, R.	Mead, M.
Bauer, R.A.	Havelock, R.G.	Miles, M.B.
Becker, H.S.	Hopkins, R.	Mouton, J.S.
Beckhard, R.	Hornstein, H.A.	Rogers, C.R.
Bell, D.	Katz, E.	Schein, E.H.
Blake, R.R.	Kelly, G.A.	Schiavo, R.S.
Calder, P.H.	Kelman, H.C.	Shepard, H.A.
Callahan, D.M.	Klein, D.C.	Sloma, R.L.
Caplan, G.	Lawrence, P.	Trist, E.L.
Clark, J.V.	Leeds, R.	Walton, R.E.
Davis, S.A.	Lippitt, R.	Watson, G.
Ferguson, C.K.	Lorsch, J.W.	Winn, A.

Topics

Change Mechanisms	Opinion Change
Change Strategy	Problem Solving
Conflict/Conflict Resolution	Resistance to Change
Consultant	Sociotechnical Systems
Diagnosis/Evaluation	Survey Feedback
Ethics	Values

Burke, W. Warner, ed. CONTEMPORARY ORGANIZATION DEVELOPMENT:
CONCEPTUAL ORIENTATIONS AND INTERVENTIONS. Washington, D.C.:
NTL Institute for Applied Behavioral Science, 1972. 276 p.

This volume presents papers from twenty-three authors describing what they see as new technologies in organization development. These papers summarize the authors' presentations at a National Training Laboratories' two-day conference.

Contents

Section I. Conceptual Orientations to Organization Development
Section II. Structural Interventions
Section III. Interventions to Cope with Manpower Reductions and Demotions
Section IV. Training Interventions

Contributing Authors

Albertson, D.R.	King, D.C.
Blake, R.R.	Lehner, G.F.
Blumberg, A.	Lippitt, G.L.
Carrigan, S.B.	Luke, R.A., Jr.
Dyer, W.G.	Mead, W.R.
Ferguson, C.K.	Mouton, J.S.
Gibb, J.R.	Muzenrider, R.
Glidwell, J.C.	Oshry, B.
Golembiewski, R.T.	Runkel, P.J.
Hall, J.	Schmuck, R.A.
Harvey, J.B.	Sherwood, J.J.
Herman, S.M.	

Topics

Change Strategy   Intervention
Change Technology

Burke, W. Warner, and Hornstein, Harvey A., eds. THE SOCIAL TECHNOLOGY OF ORGANIZATION DEVELOPMENT. Fairfax, Va.: NTL Learning Resources Corp., 1972. 340 p.

Twenty-one readings, along with brief introductory comments from the editors, comprise this volume. The majority of the readings are organized in sections according to the editors' classification of five major types of OD interventions: team-building, managing conflict, technostructural intervention, data feedback, and training.

Contents

Section I: Overview
 What, Not Again! Manage People Better?, Marvin R. Weisbord
 Organization Development in Public Agencies: Perspectives on Theory and Practice, Robert T. Golembiewski
 Some Reflections on the Organization Development and Consultation Process Within Religious Organizations, James D. Anderson
 Successful Entry as a Key to Successful Organization Development in Big City School Systems, C. Brooklyn Derr

Topics

Action Research
Attitude/Attitude Change
Change Strategy
Change Technology
Conflict/Conflict Resolution

Job Enrichment
Laboratory Training
Survey Feedback
Team Building/Development
Third Party

Dalton, Gene W.; Lawrence, Paul R.; and Greiner, Larry E. ORGANIZA-
TIONAL CHANGE AND DEVELOPMENT. Homewood, Ill.: Irwin-Dorsey,
1970. 393 p.

This book contains a series of case studies and readings which focus
on organizational change. Many of the readings are partially or
fully reprinted from previously published works.

Contents

Introduction
    Organization Change and Development, L.E. Greiner
        and L.B. Barnes
Cases
    Dashman Company
    Superior State Quarry, Parts 1 and 2
    The Gordon Company
    Battleship "Y"
    The Metro Bottling Company
    Randley Stories, Inc., A & B
    Simmonds Precision Products
    TRW Systems Group, A, B, & C
    New England Mutual, A, B, & C
    The Arrow Company
Readings
    How to Deal with Resistance to Change, P.R. Lawrence
    Applied Organization Change in Industry: Structural,
        Technical and Human Approaches, H.J. Leavitt
    Patterns of Organizational Change, L.E. Greiner
    A Psychologist Looks at Executive Development, H.
        Levinson
    The Confrontation Meeting, R. Beckhard
    Breakthrough in Organization Development, R.R. Blake,
        J.S. Mouton, L.B. Barnes, and L.E. Greiner
    T-Groups for Organizational Effectiveness, C. Argyris
    Giving and Receiving Feedback, J. Anderson
    Laboratory Education: Impact on People and Organiza-
        tions, M.D. Dunnette and J.P. Campbell
    Motivation and Behavior, G.H. Litwin and R.A. Stringer,
        Jr.
    Suggested List for Further Reading in Organizational
        Change and Development

Contributing Authors

Anderson, J.	Blake, R.R.	Levinson, H.
Argyris, C.	Campbell, J.P.	Litwin, G.H.
Barnes, L.B.	Dunnette, M.D.	Mouton, J.S.
Beckhard, R.	Leavitt, H.J.	Stringer, R.A.

Topics

Change Strategy   Managerial Grid
Confrontation   Motivation
Feedback   Organization Effectiveness
Laboratory Training   Resistance to Change
Management Training/Development   T-Groups

Marrow, Alfred J., ed. THE FAILURE OF SUCCESS. New York: AMACOM, 1972. viii, 339 p.

A combination of case studies, theoretical pieces, and descriptions are presented "to illustrate a point: Management methods based on sound psychological principles have provided workable answers for American industry in the still-too-rare instances where they have been used with commitment and seriousness" (p. 9).

Contents

For the Puzzled Executive/A Briefing
Part One: Organizations and the Quality of Life
   A Few Words in Advance, Chris Argyris
   The Failure of Success, Alfred J. Marrow
   Imaginative New Ways to Create Satisfying Jobs, Judson Gooding
   Organizational Stress and Individual Strain, John R.P. French and Robert D. Caplan
   Problems that Worry Executives, Harry Levinson
Part Two: Harnessing the Skills of Behavioral Science
   Participation: How it Works, Alfred J. Marrow
   The Effect of Participation on Performance, Alfred J. Marrow
   Managing Major Change, Alfred J. Marrow, Stanley E. Seashore, and David G. Bowers
   Does Organizational Change Last?, Stanley E. Seashore and David G. Bowers
   What Makes a Work Group Successful.?, Edward E. Lawler III and Cortlandt Cammann
Part Three: Releasing Human Potential
   Introduction/The Right Man in the Right Job
J.C. Penney Company
   How a Scientific Assessment Center Works, William C. Byham
American Telephone and Telegraph Company
   Studying Careers and Assessing Ability, Douglas W. Bray, Donald L. Grant, and Richard J. Campbell
   What We Ask of Behavioral Scientists, William C. Mercer

Topics

ATTITUDES, NORMS, AND VALUES

Alderfer, Clayton P. "Effect of Individual, Group, and Intergroup Relations on Attitudes toward a Management Development Program." JOURNAL OF AP-PLIED PSYCHOLOGY 55, no. 4 (1971): 302-11.

This study, which investigated attitudes concerning a management development program in a bank, indicated that such attitudes were a function of both individual (e.g., pay satisfaction, seniority) and group level variables (e.g., employment group membership).

Topics

Attitude/Attitude Change   Management Training Develop-
                                            ment

_____. "The HERWEGA EFFECT in Organizational Change." Technical Report to the Office of Naval Research, 1974.

Reactions to and involvement in one intervention (job enrichment) were used as predictors of attitudes toward a second and subsequent intervention (Communications Group). The results indicate that attitudes toward the second intervention "could be understood partially as a function of whether he/she had participated in job enrichment and how he/she felt about that experience." The implications of these findings are discussed with respect to dealing with reactions from previous interventions prior to the implementation on new programs.

Topics

Attitude Change   Consultant
Change Agent   Resistance to Change

Argyris, Chris [A.]. "Interpersonal Barriers to Decision-making." HARVARD BUSINESS REVIEW 44, no. 2 (1966): 84-97.

Argyris identifies an incongruency between the norms (innovation, risk taking, flexibility, and trust in the executive system) that top managers suggest are the basis for effective decision making and actual behavior. The consequences of this lack of congruence include restricted commitment, subordinate gamesmanship, lack of awareness, the withholding of negative feelings toward superiors, distrust and antagonism, and poor interactions. These factors are seen as impeding good decision making. It is suggested further that the forces operating against good decision making operate most strongly when the most important decisions are faced.

Topics

Commitment   Management
Decision Making   Norms
Flexibility   Risk/Risk-Taking
Innovation   Trust

_____. "Interpersonal Competence and Organizational Effectiveness." In his
INTERPERSONAL COMPETENCE AND ORGANIZATIONAL EFFECTIVENESS, pp.
38-54. Homewood, Ill.: Irwin, 1962.

According to the model presented, these values of formal organization lead to decreased organizational effectiveness: "(1) The relevant human relationships are those related to the organizational objective; (2) human relations effectiveness increases as behavior is
rational, logical, and clearly communicated. Personal attitudes,
feelings, and values tend to decrease effectiveness; (3) Human relations are most effectively influenced through direction, coercions,
and control as well as rewards and penalties that serve to emphasize the rational behavior and getting the job done."

Argyris notes that increasing interpersonal competence is a necessary but not sufficient step in increasing organizational effectiveness. Values also must be altered to support changes in organizational, technological, and interpersonal factors.

Topics

Formal Organization   Organization Effectiveness
Interpersonal Competence   Values

_____. PERSONALITY AND ORGANIZATION: THE CONFLICT BETWEEN
SYSTEM AND THE INDIVIDUAL. New York: Harper & Row, 1957. 291 p.

The basic proposition of this book is that a mismatch exists between
the principles of formal organization and the needs of healthy individuals. This incongruity increases as (1) the employees increase
in maturity, (2) as the formal structure is more clear-cut and logi-
cally tight for maximum formal organizational effectiveness, (3)
as one goes down in the line of command, and (4) as the jobs become more mechanized. The results of the mismatch are conflict,
frustration, and failure on the part of organizational members. Each
of these negative results is decreased, however, through the informal organization. The work concludes that the apparently incongruent behavior of the employees coerced by the informal organization is necessary if healthy individuals are to maintain a minimum
level of health and if the formal organization is to obtain optimum
expression of its demands.

Contents

1. Basic assumptions and viewpoints of the book
2. The human personality
3. The formal organization
4. Individual and group adaptation
5. Management's reaction and its impact upon the employees
6. The first-line supervisor
7. Decreasing the degree of incongruence between the formal organization

8. The development of effective executive behavior
9. Summary and conclusions

Topics

Adaptation
Adjustment
Formal Organization

Individual-Organization Inter-
face
Informal Organization
Leadership

Kelman, Herbert C. "Process of Opinion Change." PUBLIC OPINION QUAR-
TERLY 25, no. 1 (1961): 57-78.

Three processes of opinion change are identified and elaborated.
Compliance occurs when an individual accepts influence from another
person or from a group because he hopes to achieve a favorable
reaction from the other. Identification occurs when an individual
adopts behavior derived from another person or a group because this
behavior is associated with a satisfying self-defining relationship
to this person or group. Internalization occurs when an individual
accepts influence because the induced behavior is congruent with
his value system.

Comparisons are made between the three processes, focusing on
antecedents and consequents associated with each.

Topics

Compliance
Identification
Influence

Internalization
Opinion Change

Lawler, Edward E. III. "Job Attitudes and Employee Motivation: Theory, Research and Practice." PERSONNEL PSYCHOLOGY 23, no. 2 (1970): 223-37.

The author offers six suggestions for affecting attitudes and performance which are derived from the expectancy model of motivation.

Topics

Attitude/Attitude Change
Expectancy Theory
Motivation

Performance
Reward System
Satisfaction

McGregor, Douglas. THE HUMAN SIDE OF ENTERPRISE. New York: McGraw-
Hill, 1960. 246 p.

The major emphasis in this book is on managerial strategies, especially the assumptions and consequences related to two distinct
strategies--Theory X and Theory Y. According to McGregor the
latter is associated with effective managerial behavior.

Additional topics include some general notions regarding learning,
especially learning through T-groups, and characteristics of efficient

and inefficient groups.

Contents

Part One: The Theoretical Assumptions of Management
1. Management and scientific knowledge
2. Methods of influence and control
3. Theory X: The traditional view of direction and control
4. Theory Y: The integration of individual and organizational goals

Part Two: Theory Y in Practice
5. Management by integration and self-control
6. A critique of performance appraisal
7. Administering salaries and promotions
8. The Scanlon Plan
9. Participation in perspective
10. The managerial climate
11. Staff-line relationships
12. Improving staff-line collaboration

Part Three: The Development of Managerial Talent
13. An analysis of leadership
14. Management development programs
15. Acquiring managerial skills in the classroom
16. The managerial team

Topics

Goals (Individual/Organizational)	Participation
Group Processes	Scanlon Plan
Leadership	T-Group
Learning	Theory X
Management	Theory Y

Marrow, Alfred J., and French, John R.P., Jr. "Changing a Stereotype in Industry." JOURNAL OF SOCIAL ISSUES 1, no. 3 (1945): 33-37.

The authors report a study in which an attempt was made to change attitudes toward older female workers through participation of management in research and supervisors in group discussion and decision.

The authors conclude from the study that "through a process of guided experiences which are equally his own, a person may be reoriented so that he gradually takes on within himself the attitudes which he would not accept from others."

Topics

Attitude/Attitude Change	Stereotype
Participation	

Rogers, Carl [R.]. "Interpersonal Relationships: Year 2000." JOURNAL OF APPLIED BEHAVIORAL SCIENCE 4, no. 3 (1968): 265-80.

Rogers suggests that in the future industries will be devoting as
much attention to "the quality of interpersonal relationships and
the quality of communications" as is now given to technology.
This will particularly result from the recognition that organizational
growth and development can be realized only through a facilitation
of individual growth and fulfillment.

Topics

Communications   Interpersonal Processes
Individual Growth

Schmidt, Warren H., ed. ORGANIZATIONAL FRONTIERS AND HUMAN
VALUES. Belmont, Calif.: Wadsworth, 1970. 190 p.

The major focus of this book is the nature of organizations as they
will be in the future. The variety of organizations discussed includes schools, corporations, and societies.

Contents

Part One: An Overview, W.H. Schmidt
    1. View at the frontier
    2. The revolutionary 1970s
    3. The new organizational frontiersman: The leader-learner
Part Two: Summary of the Organizational Frontiers Seminar, C.R.
           Price
    4. Between cultures: The current crisis of transition
    5. Living through the transition
    6. Managing organizations in a time of crisis
Part Three: Selected Readings
    7. Assessment and perspective, J.V. Lindsay
    8. Is it always right to be right? W.H. Schmidt
    9. Urban North America: The challenge of the next
       thirty years, E.L. Trist
   10. The university as an organizational frontier, J.M.
       Elden, R. Goldstone, and M.K. Brown
   11. Student protest as a resource for corporate planning
       and development, S.A. Culbert and J.M. Elden
   12. American management: Everybody's business, H.M.
       Williams
   13. Values, man, and organizations, R. Tannenbaum and
       S.A. Davis
   14. Primary target for change: The manager or the orga-
       nization?, W.W. Burke and W.H. Schmidt
Part Four: Looking Further
   15. Review at the frontier, W.H. Schmidt
   16. Seventy probably major domestic, nonmilitary trends
       and events in 1980, G.A. Steiner
   17. Annotated bibliography, Jean-Marie Toulouse
   18. Bibliography on organization development

Topics

Crisis	Management
Future Organizations	Protest
Leadership	Values

Tannenbaum, Robert, and Davis, Sheldon A. "Values, Man, and Organizations." In ORGANIZATIONAL FRONTIERS AND HUMAN VALUES, edited by
W.H. Schmidt, pp. 129-49. Belmont, Calif.: Wadsworth, 1970.

This article describes a shift in values that the authors suggest is
taking place in organizational settings. The shift is attributed to
movement away from bureaucratic organizational forms and towards
forms of organization that recognize individuality.

Topics

Collaboration	Power
Competition	Process Work
Confrontation	Risk/Risk-Taking
Feedback	Status
Individuality	Trust
Organization Forms	Values

Walton, Richard E., and Warwick, Donald P. "The Ethics of Organization
Development." JOURNAL OF APPLIED BEHAVIORAL SCIENCE 9, no. 6 (1973):
681-98.

"Many of the ethical dilemmas in OD fall under three generic
headings: power, freedom, and professional responsibility" (p. 683).
Within the context of these three areas the authors reflect on current practices, including potential and actual abuses, and incon-
gruities which exist between the stated values and the actual behaviors of OD practitioners.

Topics

Consultation	Manipulation
Ethics	Values

GROUP PROCESSES

Benne, Kenneth D., and Sheats, Paul. "Functional Roles of Group Members."
JOURNAL OF SOCIAL ISSUES 4, no. 2 (1948): 41-49.

Three groupings of member roles are identified and elaborated.
Early NTL T-groups provided the population studied. The groupings
are group task roles, group building and maintenance roles, and
individual roles. Each grouping includes several specific roles.
Group task roles include initiator-contributor; information seeker;
opinion seeker; information giver; elaborator; coordinator; orienter;
evaluator-critic; energizer; procedural technician; and recorder.

Group building and maintenance roles include encourager; harmo-
nizer; compromiser; gatekeeper and expediter; standard setter or ego
ideal; group observer and commentator; and follower. Individual
roles include aggressor; blocker; recognition seeker; self-confessor;
playboy; dominator; help seeker; and special interest pleader.

Topics

Group Roles   T-Group

Bennis, Warren G., and Shepard, Herbert A. "A Theory of Group Development." HUMAN RELATIONS 9 (1956): 415-37.

The theory presented is based on experience from T-groups. Group
development is seen as involving "the overcoming of obstacles to
valid communication among the members, or the development of
methods for achieving and testing consensus." Two major phases
of group development are suggested: dependence and interdependence. "During the authority ('dependence') phase, the group
moves from preoccupation with submission to preoccupation with
rebellion to resolution of the dependence problem. Within the
personal (or 'interdependence') phase the group moves from a preoccupation with inter-member identification to a preoccupation
with individual identity to a resolution of the interdependence
problem."

Each of the major phases consists of three subphases. Dependence
includes: dependence-flight, counterdependence-flight, and resolution-
catharsis. Interdependence consists of enchantment-flight,
disenchantment-flight, and consensual validation.

Topics

Group Development   T-Group

Cartwright, Dorwin. "Achieving Change in People: Some Applications of
Group Dynamics Theory." HUMAN RELATIONS 4 (1951): 381-93. (Also in
E.P. Hollander and R.G. Hunt, eds., CURRENT PERSPECTIVES IN SOCIAL
PSYCHOLOGY. New York: Oxford University Press, 1967, pp. 520-29.)

This article cites several important studies in support of a number
of principles pertaining to the group as a medium and target of
change.

Topics

Group Change   Group Processes
Group Influence

Coch, Lester, and French, John R.P., Jr. "Overcoming Resistance to Change."
HUMAN RELATIONS 1, no. 4 (1948): 512-33.

This article reports a classic study in which participation was used
as a means of solving problems caused by changing methods of pro-

duction. The problems included high turnover, low efficiency, restricted output, and aggression against management.

Three groups of employees were matched for change, efficiency, and cohesiveness. Each group participated to a different degree in the change. Members of one group were merely told about the changes and why they were needed to participate in the decision-making process ("Representative-participation" group). All members of the third group participated in the decision-making process ("Total-participation" group).

It was found that "the rate of recovery is directly proportional to the amount of participation, and that the rates of turnover and aggression are inversely proportional to the amount of participation."

Topics

Participation   Resistance to Change
Problem Solving

Friedlander, Frank. "The Primacy of Trust as a Facilitator of Further Group Accomplishment." JOURNAL OF APPLIED BEHAVIORAL SCIENCE 6, no. 4 (1970): 387-400.

This study set out to explore the extent to which intragroup trust is a necessary prerequisite to further group accomplishment.

"Results indicate that prelaboratory trust is a key predictor of eventual group accomplishment, although trust itself did not increase as a result of an isolated laboratory training experience. Furthermore, and as a function of training, the trainee's post-laboratory concept of trust merged with his concept of an effective group and an effective group meeting," the author writes.

The author suggests that efforts must be made to build trust prior to a laboratory experience to facilitate increases in group effectiveness. (See also Friedlander, pp. 65 and 132, and J.R. Gibb, below.)

Topics

Group Development   Laboratory Training
Group Effectiveness   Organizational Training Labo-
Group Processes   ratory
                              Trust

Gibb, Jack R. "Climate for Trust Formation." In T-GROUP THEORY AND LABORATORY METHOD, edited by Leland P. Bradford, Jack R. Gibb, and Kenneth D. Benne, pp. 279-309. New York: John Wiley, 1964.

Gibb hypothesizes four modal concerns affecting all social interactions. "Group formation occurs as a containing set of solutions to the problems deriving from the four focal concerns of acceptance, data, goal, and control."

A model is presented based on the four primary modal concerns, derivatives of the modal concerns, symptoms of unresolved concern, and symptoms of resolved concern.

(See also Friedlander, above.)

Topics

Group Development   Trust

Lewin, Kurt. "Frontiers in Group Dynamics: Concept, Method, and Reality in Social Equilibria and Social Change." HUMAN RELATIONS 1 (1947): 5-41.

The force field approach to the analysis is presented. Lewin suggests that to encourage change, one can increase forces toward change or decrease the forces against change. In any change effort the whole force field must be considered.

The group as a force for or against individual change is examined. "As long as group values are unchanged the individual will resist changes more strongly the farther he is to depart from group standards. If the group standard itself is change, the resistance which is due to the relation between individual and group standard is eliminated."

Three stages of successful change are described. These are "unfreezing" the group from its present level, "moving" to a new level, and "freezing" group life at the new level.

Topics

Change Phases   Group Processes
Change Processes   Resistance to Change
Force Field   Unfreezing
Freezing

Luft, Joseph. GROUP PROCESSES. Palo Alto, Calif.: National Press Books, 1970. 122 p.

This short volume presents a brief review of many aspects of group processes. The author draws from the works of many persons but places major emphasis on the laboratory approach to studying group dynamics.

Contents

1. Group processes: An introduction to group dynamics
2. Elements of laboratory methods for studying group processes
3. The Johari Window: A graphic model of awareness in interpersonal relations
4. Basic issues in group processes
5. Interaction patterns and metacommunication
6. Group processes and organizational behavior
7. Group processes and clinical psychology
8. The teacher and group processes
9. Current trends

Topics

Group Development
Group Processes
Johari Window
Laboratory Approach

Leadership
Metacommunication Theory
Transfer of Training

Tuckman, Bruce W. "Developmental Sequence in Small Groups." PSYCHO-LOGICAL BULLETIN 63, no. 6 (1965): 384-99.

A review is presented of fifty articles which cover groups in four settings: therapy groups, T-groups, natural groups, and laboratory groups.

Developmental stages of groups are identified in both the social and task realms.

Topics

Cohesion
Conflict/Conflict Resolution
Emotionality
Group Development
Group Processes

Laboratory Group
Role
Task
T-Group
Therapy

THE PRACTICE OF ORGANIZATION DEVELOPMENT

Consultancy

Aram, John D., and Stoner, James A.F. "Development of an Organizational Change Role." JOURNAL OF APPLIED BEHAVIORAL SCIENCE 8, no. 4 (1972): 438-49.

The careers of nine U.S. business school graduates in organizations in Colombia, South America were studies from the perspective of establishing organizational change roles. The investigation was based on data obtained from four three- to ten-hour interviews conducted during a year and a half period. The following conclusions from this study seem justified as propositions for a theory of developing organizational change roles: (1) congruent initial expectations between individual and organization and an initial adaptive entry style are necessary conditions for individual satisfaction with and continuation of one's role; (2) behavioral style tends toward independence in situations of incongruent initial expectations, though independent behavior can have a different impact later in the organizational role; (3) the most influential change role comes through a combination of high congruency of expectations, an adaptive style, and the gaining of influence through administrative authority; (4) other types of role influence--expertise and personal--are dependent on the receptivity and personal outlook, respectively, of other organizational members.

Topics

Adaptation	Consultant
Change Agent	Expectations
Change Strategy	Role

Benne, Kenneth D.; Chin, Robert; and Bennis, Warren G. "Science and Practice." In THE PLANNING OF CHANGE, edited by Warren G. Bennis, Kenneth D. Benne, and Robert Chin, pp. 113-23. New York: Holt, Rinehart and Winston, 1969.

> Some problems of the social scientist in the role of a change agent are explored. The authors note that for such persons the luxury of studying completed events is not available. The change agent is described as a person who must be able to diagnose and intervene in ongoing events in such a way as to "maximize the valid human values implicit in the events."
>
> Change agentry is described as an artistic skill requiring the use of feelings and emotions in addition to conceptual frameworks.

Topics

Change Agent	Skill
Diagnosis/Evaluation	Values
Intervention	

Browne, Philip J., and Cotton, Chester C. "Marginality, A Force for the OD Practitioner." TRAINING AND DEVELOPMENT JOURNAL, April 1975, pp. 14-18.

> Benefits and liabilities associated with the marginality position (e.g., being a part of both the client system and the professional world) of OD practitioners are briefly cited.

Topics

| Change Agent | Third Party |
| Consultant | |

Ferguson, Charles K. "Concerning the Nature of Human Systems and the Consultant's Role." JOURNAL OF APPLIED BEHAVIORAL SCIENCE 4, no. 2 (1968): 179-93.

> "A consultant does much the same thing whether he is working with one person, a small group, or a large organization. He uses himself to help a client system to externalize, to explicate 'non-fit' between interfaces or along boundaries. He uses himself to release forces that move toward balance or health in human systems of any size. He is always an aide or an instrument; he should not be a principal or an essential member party. He precipitates a process the substance of which comes from the members.
>
> "The consultant can do any of the following to fulfill his role:

capture data, scan for troubled interfaces, promote psychological bonding, act and analyze process, clarify formulation of issues, release emotional pressures, make communication congruent, encourage feedback, serve as plumber and/or obstetrician, promote a spirit of inquiry, analyze ongoing process, coach and build teams, assist in the management of conflict, promote a proper psychological climate, take calculated risks."

Topics

Change Agent	Consultant
Communications	Feedback
Conflict/Conflict Resolution	Linkage

Friedlander, Frank. "A Comparative Study of Consulting Processes and Group Development." JOURNAL OF APPLIED BEHAVIORAL SCIENCE 4, no. 4 (1968): 377-400.

"Results indicate that the success of the development programs could be much better explained by whether there were prelaboratory and postlaboratory consultant activities than by variations in trainer role and behavior or by differences in content and climate of training sessions," the author concludes.

An approach which integrated pre- and post-laboratory work and utilized internal consulting groups to facilitate data gathering and action steps resulted in outstanding group growth.

This is a partial report of a study in a 6,000 member R&D facility of the armed services. Twelve work groups were involved. (See also Friedlander, pp. 61 and 132.)

Topics

Consultant	Organizational Training Labo-
Group Development	ratory
	Trainer

Havelock, Ronald G., and Havelock, Mary C. TRAINING FOR CHANGE AGENTS: A GUIDE TO THE DESIGN OF TRAINING PROGRAMS IN EDUCATION AND OTHER FIELDS. Ann Arbor, Mich.: Institute for Social Research, 1973. 249 p.

This book is directed toward change agents and change agent trainers in education and in other human service areas where specialized resource helping and linking roles are being developed. The book is divided into two major sections, the first emphasizing "the theory, goals, and structure essential to program design" and the second "how model training programs could be put together for various types of objectives" (p. 4).

Contents

Introduction
Chapter I: Our Contemporary Knowledge of the Change Process

Topics

Change Agent	Feedback
Communication	Group Processes
Conflict/Conflict Resolution	Laboratory Training
Consultant	Problem Solving
Consultation	Role
Diagnosis/Evaluation	Transfer of training
Education	Values

Kolb, David A., and Boyatzis, Richard E. "On the Dynamics of the Helping Relationship." JOURNAL OF APPLIED BEHAVIORAL SCIENCE 6, no. 3 (1970): 267-89.

The authors attempt to describe the type of individual who makes an effective helper, defining this person as one who, "in an environment where giving help is seen as appropriate (the T-Group), attempts to help others while the others see this help as significant and important to them."

"A conceptual framework of helping relationships is presented which includes the nature of the task, the helper, the receiver of help, the environment and psychological climate of the relationship, and the information feedback which occurs during the relationship."

The authors studied eight T-groups of the "self-directed change" type. Each participant had a change goal and the task of helping others achieve their personal change goals.

All participants completed a semantic differential instrument and a six-picture TAT. At the conclusion of each session each group member completed a form describing feedback given and received.

Statistically significant differences suggest that "ineffective helpers are differentiated from effective helpers and nonhelpers by very high n Achievement and n Power scores and very low n Affiliation scores. In this experiment none of the three motives significantly differentiates effective helpers from nonhelpers."

Topics

Change Agent	Semantic Differential
Feedback	TAT
Helper	T-Group
Self-Change	Trainer

Kolb, David A., and Frohman, Alan L. "An Organizational Development Approach to Consulting." SLOAN MANAGEMENT REVIEW, Fall 1970, pp. 51-65.

This article describes a seven-stage model for planned change focusing on two primary issues: the relationship between client and consultant and the nature of the work. The stages included in the model are: scouting, entry, diagnosis, planning, action, evaluation, and termination. Each stage is briefly elaborated and "normal" and "arrested" development are described.

Topics

Change Agent   Entry
Consultant   Scouting
Diagnosis/Evaluation   Termination

Pettigrew, Andrew M. "Towards a Political Theory of Organizational Intervention." HUMAN RELATIONS 28, no. 3 (1975): 191-208.

The author suggests that the internal consultants' ability to influence clients will be a function of his possession and tactical use of five power resources: expertise, control over information, political access and sensitivity, assessed stature, and group support. The first three are suggested as necessary but not sufficient for consultant power. Beyond these the consultants' ability to negotiate and persuade "depends on his assessed stature with the appropriate figures in his political network" (p. 191).

Topics

Change Agent   Power
Consultant

Steele, Fred I. "Consultants and Detectives." JOURNAL OF APPLIED BEHAVIORAL SCIENCE 5, no. 2 (1969): 187-202.

Potential dangers inherent in the consultant role are described. These dangers relate to satisfying attributes of the consultant's role which can impede attainment of the major goal of improving the capabilities and functioning of the client system. These attributes include the temporary nature of involvement in a system; the focus on gathering evidence and trying to solve the puzzles which it represents; the potential for dramatics; the potential action orientation and the excitement it contains; the status of "expert" in behavioral science; and the stimulation of working on several cases simultaneously.

Steele suggests that demands placed upon the consultant can help guard against the potentially negative consequences of these attributes. These demands are promotion of consciousness of self; avoidance of incorporation into the client system; use of some collaborator or sounding board with whom to check perceptions, ideas, and feelings; use of intuition as one means of generating ways to understand the situation; and avoidance of the tendency to lump people into the oversimplified categories of good and bad.

Topics

Change Agent   Diagnosis/Evaluation
Consultant   Valid Information

_____. CONSULTING FOR ORGANIZATIONAL CHANGE. Amherst: University of Massachusetts Press, 1975. 200 p.

A learning process for both consultants and their clients is the major organizing theme for this exploration of consultation.

Contents

1. The Consulting Function
2. Learning from Consulting
3. Learning and the Client's Role
4. Organizational Overlearning
5. Using the Laboratory Method to Train Consultants and Clients
6. The Compleat Consultant's Costume Catalogue
7. Teamwork in Consultation
8. Consultants and Detectives
9. The Scene of the Crime
10. Learning and Designing

Topics

Consultant   Learning
Consultation   Team Building/Development
Laboratory Approach   T-Group
Laboratory Training

Tichy, Noel M. "Agents of Planned Social Change." ADMINISTRATIVE SCIENCE QUARTERLY 19, no. 2 (1974): 164-82.

Questionnaire data gathered from ninety-one social-change agents were used to classify strategies for change and examine contradictions or incongruencies in change models affecting change agent practices. The four strategies or change agent types were identified as outside-pressure, organization development, people-change technology, and analysis for the top.

An exploration of the congruence between values and actions, cognitions and actions reveal some substantial inconsistencies. For example, the organization development change agents "have a value-oriented change approach as reflected in their goals, but they are generally employed by organizations not for these values, but to help with problems effecting efficiency and output" (p. 179).

The advantages of congruence are described in terms of moving toward a science through "(1) making the change agents' model assumptions and values explicit; (2) changing values of clients and change agents toward accepting innovations as opportunities to learn about social change through evaluation research; and (3) increasing evaluation research on competing intervention strategies" (p. 182).

Topics

Change Agent

_____. "How Different Types of Change Agents Diagnose Organizations."
HUMAN RELATIONS 28, no. 9 (1975): 771-79.

This study focuses on the diagnostic strategies employed by 133
change agents and reveals differences relating to value orientations
and primary change techniques. Interviews and questionnaires were
used to examine "(1) subcategories or specific pieces of information
[change agents] seek in a diagnosis; (2) the major categories of information sought during diagnosis; and (3) the relationship of the
diagnostic categories to interventions" (p. 776). The results indicate identifiable differences in diagnostic focus associated with each
of four classifications of change agent types.

Topics

Change Agent   Diagnosis/Evaluation
Change Strategy   Values
Change Technology

Diagnosis and Evaluation

Alderfer, Clayton P. "Organizational Diagnosis from Initial Client Reactions
to a Researcher." HUMAN ORGANIZATION 27 (1968): 260-65.

Meetings were held with key organizational managers to discuss a
field study in which organizational members were to participate.
Behavior of the managers was used to predict behavior (attendance
at future meetings) and attitude (satisfaction with respect by superiors) differences in subordinates. Four types of managers were
distinguished on the basis of the presence or absence of "threat"
and "fantasy." The types are distinguished as follows:

Type	Threat	Fantasy
Pilot	Present	Present
Producer	Present	Absent
Checker	Absent	Present
Leveler	Absent	Absent

Attendance of subordinates at the first meeting was found to be
related to perceived threat by the manager. Where threat was
judged to be present (Pilot and Producer), satisfaction with respect
by superiors was found to be related to fantasy. Persons from departments headed by supervisors exhibiting fantasy (Pilot and Check-
er) were less satisfied with respect by superiors than those in which
the supervisor did not exhibit fantasy (Producer and Leveler).

The author suggests that this study supports the idea that organizational resistance can be determined from initial interactions between
the researcher and members of the organization to be studied.

Topics

Absence   Fantasy
Attendance   Resistance to Change
Diagnosis/Evaluation   Threat

Benedict, Barbara A., et al. "The Clinical-Experimental Approach to Assessing Organizational Change Efforts." JOURNAL OF APPLIED BEHAVIORAL SCIENCE 2, no. 3 (1967): 347-80.

A model is presented for evaluating organizational change efforts calling for "the separation of researcher and change agent roles, the construction and testing of general and specific clinical hypotheses, thorough-going experimental design, and careful documentation of change-agent assumptions, plans, strategies and effects." The authors argue that data-collection activities must be both clinical and experimental and should include a natural-history account of events which occur before, during, and after the intervention.

The method was used to assess changes in a school system resulting from a four-day off-site meeting with thirty-two members of the administrative staff. These same people also participated in a series of six meetings held over a six-week period. No changes were reported as a result of the change effort.

Topics

Change Agent   Diagnosis/Evaluation
Clinical-Experimental Approach Researcher
Data Collection

Hackman, J. Richard, and Oldham, Greg R. "Development of the Job Diagnostic Survey." JOURNAL OF APPLIED PSYCHOLOGY 60, no. 2 (1975): 159-70.

The authors describe the Job Diagnostic Survey as an attempt (a) to diagnose existing jobs to determine if (and how) they might be redesigned and (b) to evaluate the effects of job changes on employees. The survey measures (a) objective job dimensions, (b) individual psychological states, (c) affective reactions of employees to the job and work setting, and (d) individual growth need strength.

Topics

Absence   Job Enrichment
Autonomy   Motivation
Feedback   Satisfaction
Job Design   Turnover
Job Diagnostic Survey

Harris, Chester W., ed. PROBLEMS IN MEASURING CHANGE. Madison: University of Wisconsin Press, 1967. 259 p.

Organization Development: Background, Overview

These twelve conference papers focus on the measurement of change.
Most of the papers were prepared by individuals with strong backgrounds in psychometrics.

Contents

1. Some Persisting Dilemmas in the Measurement of Change, Carl Bereiter
2. Elementary Models for Measuring Change, Frederic M. Lord
3. The Reliability of Changes Measured by Mental Test Scores, Harold Webster and Carl Bereiter
4. Univariate Analysis of Variance Procedures in the Measurement of Change, John Gaito and David E. Wiley
5. Multivariate Analysis of Variance of Repeated Measurements, R. Darrell Bock
6. Multivariate Models for Evaluating Change, Paul Horst
7. Implications of Factor Analysis of Three-Way Matrices for Measurement of Change, Ledyard R. Tucker
8. Canonical Factor Models for the Description of Change, Chester W. Harris
9. Image Analysis, Henry F. Kaiser
10. The Structuring of Change by P-Technique and Incremental R-Technique, Raymond B. Cattell
11. Statistical Models for the Study of Change in the Single Case, Wayne H. Holtzman
12. From Description to Experimentation: Interpreting Trends as Quasi-Experiments, Donald T. Campbell

Topics

Action Research
Diagnosis/Evaluation

Research Designs

Nadler, David A., et al., eds. MICHIGAN ORGANIZATIONAL ASSESSMENT PACKAGE: PROGRESS REPORT II. Ann Arbor, Mich.: Institute for Social Research, 1975.

This monograph presents a collection of techniques designed to measure the effectiveness of approaches developed to enhance productivity and quality of work life.

Topics

Attitude/Attitude Change
Group Processes
Influence
Job Design
Leadership

Michigan Organizational
Assessment Package
Role
Satisfaction
Technology

Taylor, James C., and Bowers, David G. SURVEY OF ORGANIZATIONS: A MACHINE-SCORED STANDARDIZED QUESTIONNAIRE INSTRUMENT. Ann Arbor, Mich.: Institute for Social Research, 1972. 165 p.

A monograph summarizing the evidence which the Organizational

Development Research Program (Institute for Social Research, University of Michigan) has concerning the Survey of Organizations questionnaire. The volume is a questionnaire manual providing detailed information on the development, composition, reliability, and validity of the instrument.

Contents

1. Introduction: The origin of a standard questionnaire
2. The machine-scored core questionnaire
3. Question stem reversal and position response bias
4. The effect of various questionnaire modifications on responses
5. Revisions of the machine-scored questionnaire
6. Core questionnaire measurement of leadership
7. Measurements of organizational climate
8. The satisfaction and group process areas
9. Validity of the instrument
Appendix A--1967, 1968, 1969, 1970 forms of the questionnaire
Appendix B--Survey administration procedures

Topics

Climate   Satisfaction
Diagnosis/Evaluation   Survey Feedback
Group Processes   Survey of Organizations
Leadership

REVIEWS AND MULTIORGANIZATIONAL RESEARCH

Buchanan, Paul C. "Crucial Issues in Organizational Development." In SOCIAL INTERVENTION, edited by Harvey A. Hornstein et al., pp. 386-400. New York: Free Press, 1971.

Ten cases (seven successful and three unsuccessful) are examined to identify crucial issues in the OD process. Although an initial list included thirty-three issues, only three emerged as central when the successful cases were compared with those which were unsuccessful: "(1) introducing a new model of operation which the members of an organization can consider as a basis for formulating improvement goals regarding a dimension or operation which is central to the performance of the organization; (2) sequencing objectives and action steps in such a way that linkage is established between the initial point of change and other persons, parts, and dimensions of operation internal to the target system; (3) sequencing objectives and action steps in such a way that linkage is established between the initial point of change and other persons, parts, and dimensions of the external system with which the target system has important interdependency." Similarities among the successful programs included active involvement of top managers; introduction of "a model for collecting data and for diagnosing the system's needs, which could be considered by members of the system in establishing goals for improvement"; models which "concerned the problem-solving process of the organization"; changes in the kind, distribution, or amount of influence in the system; "the development of norms and of skills which facilitated a shift from relationships based on negotiation or bargaining toward relationships based on problem solving or collaboration"; and a change agent coming from outside of the target organization.

Differences among the successful cases included the kind of model introduced, the manner of model introduction, the organizational location of the change agent, and the sequencing of involvement among levels of management.

Topics

Change Agent	Change Strategy
Change Processes	Problem Solving

Cummings, T.G.; Molloy, Edmond S.; and Glen, Roy H. "Intervention Strategies for Improving the Quality of Work Life." ORGANIZATIONAL DYNAMICS, Summer 1975, pp. 52-68.

A review of fifty-seven organizational experiments serves as the basis for an analysis of planned changes in job satisfaction, productivity, and organizational design. Nine mechanisms are identified which serve as the levers for change: pay/reward systems; autonomy/discretion; support services; training; organization structure; technical/physical; task variety; information/feedback; and interpersonal/group process. Manipulation of these factors resulted in positive outcomes on five criterion variables of costs, productivity, quality, withdrawal behavior, and attitudes.

These mechanisms and outcomes are used within four change orientations: sociotechnical/autonomous work groups; job restructuring; participative management; and structural change. Each orientation is associated with differential use of the change levers and outcomes. An evaluation of these differences indicates "autonomy/discretion alone is sufficient to account for positive attitudinal results" (p. 58) and, "information/feedback, technical/physical, task variety, and interpersonal/group process jointly account for positive productivity results" (p. 59). Also noted was the fact that "information/ feedback appears to be the action lever with the single greatest impact on productivity" (p. 58).

The article concludes with strategy suggestions for using the information.

Topics

Attitude/Attitude Change	Motivation
Autonomy	Participation
Change Strategy	Reward System
Feedback	Satisfaction
Group Process	Structural Change
Job Design	Structure
Job Enrichment	Variety

Franklin, Jerome L. "Characteristics of Successful and Unsuccessful Organization Development." JOURNAL OF APPLIED BEHAVIORAL SCIENCE 12, no. 4
(1976): 471-92.

A comparison of eleven organizations with successful OD efforts
and fourteen organizations with unsuccessful efforts reveals identifiable characteristics of each type. There was no single dimension
which was either essential or sufficient to distinguish between the
successful and unsuccessful organizations. However, there were
three general differences between the two. These distinctions indicated (1) organizations which are open to and involved in adjusting
to change are more likely to be successful in their OD effort than
are those which are stable and status-quo oriented; (2) internal
change agents who are carefully selected, do not receive training
prior to these OD efforts, and who possess assessment-prescriptive
skills are most evident in the successful organizations; and (3) more
specific interests and greater commitment to the OD projects are
associated with successful change.

Implications for the manager or consultant interested in applying
these findings to maximize the likelihood of success in OD projects
are explored.

Topics

Change Agent   Feedback
Commitment   Support
Consultant   Survey Feedback
Data Collection   Values
Diagnosis/Evaluation

Friedlander, Frank, and Brown, L. Dave. "Organization Development." In
ANNUAL REVIEW OF PSYCHOLOGY, edited by M.R. Rosenzweig and L.W.
Porter, vol. 25, pp. 313-41. Palo Alto, Calif.: Annual Reviews, 1974.

This review of the organization development literature includes
sections on research issues, technostructural approaches, human
processual approaches, comparative studies of OD interventions,
and multifaceted OD. In their introductory comments, the authors
propose a framework and suggest two primary targets of interventions (people, technology) and two primary outcomes (human fulfillment, task accomplishment).

After they discuss research issues, the authors present two major
change approaches--technostructural and human processual. Technostructural approaches are divided into three subcategories--
sociotechnical systems, job design and job enlargement, job enrich-
ment--each of which is discussed and then contrasted with the other
subcategories. Among the conclusions is that performance and satisfaction will result from job enlargement and job enrichment "contingent upon the needs of the employee, his cognitive complexity,
and his cultural milieu."

The human processual approaches are also divided into three sub-

categories--survey feedback, group development intervention, intergroup relations development. Each is discussed with respect to
the available research. Among the conclusions suggested are: there
is little evidence that survey feedback alone leads to changes in
individual behavior or organizational performance, group development activities affect participants' attitudes and sometimes their
behavior, and available evidence does not provide much information about the effects of OD interventions upon the management
of intergroup relations.

Later sections consider (1) comparative studies of OD interventions
of which only one (Bowers, p. 79) is identified as actually providing
empirical evaluations of alternative interventions and (2) multifaceted OD.

Topics

Attitude/Attitude Change	Consultant	Research Designs
Behavioral Change	Group Development	Satisfaction
Change Models	Intergroup Processes	Sociotechnical
Change Strategy	Intervention	Systems
Change Technology	Job Enlargement	Survey Feedback
Climate	Job Enrichment	Technological
Conflict/Conflict	Motivation	Change
Resolution	Performance	Vertical Job
		Loading

Frohman, M.A., and Sashkin, Marshall. "The Practice of Organizational Development: A Selective Review." Technical Report to the Office of Naval
Research, Arlington, Va., 1970. (Available from Defense Documentation Center, Cameron Station, Alexandria, Va.)

The authors review the various approaches to organizational development. Among those discussed are the Managerial Grid, survey feedback, sensitivity training, and the sociotechnical systems approach.

They offer the following observations: "Systemic observations: (1)
The support and involvement of top management is a prerequisite
for successful O.D. change. (2) Organizations are complex systems
with a variety of interrelated parts. Thus, the entire system must
be exposed or at least potentially open, to the efforts of the change
agent. (3) There must be an 'inside linker' as well as an external
source of change. (4) If O.D. is to continue as an ongoing process within a system internal change resources must be developed.
Clinical observations: (1) The system involved in change must be
the source, target, and agent of change. (2) The change agent
must be familiar with a variety of conceptual orientations toward
change. (3) The change agent needs a flexible approach in both
diagnosis and treatment. He should be able to use a variety of
methods to uncover problems in the system as well as to provide
corrective steps."

Topics

Change Agent   Sociotechnical Systems
Change Processes   Support
Diagnosis/Evaluation   Survey Feedback
Managerial Grid   Treatment
Sensitivity Training

Greiner, Larry E. "Patterns of Organizational Change." HARVARD BUSINESS REVIEW 45, no. 3 (1967): 119-30.

From a review of eighteen studies of organizational change Greiner concludes that power redistribution within the structure of an organization is basic to successful development. He identifies three major approaches to the induction of change: unilateral action, sharing of power, and delegated authority.

Six phases of successful change efforts are also noted. Each phase involved a stimulus on the power structure and a reaction from the power structure.

Suggestions for future attempts at organizational change are presented. These include a plea for efforts focusing at the top as well as lower organizational levels; a deemphasis of the use of "unilateral and delegated approaches to change"; and less parochial viewpoints on the part of managers, consultants, skeptics, and researchers.

Topics

Change Processes   Power Structure
Power Redistribution

Leavitt, Harold J. "Applied Organizational Change in Industry." In HANDBOOK OF ORGANIZATIONS, edited by James G. March, pp. 1144-70. Chicago: Rand-McNally, 1965.

Distinctions are made between structural, technological, and people approaches to change. The people approach is further divided into "manipulative" and "power-equalization" (PE) approaches. Leavitt stresses the latter in this chapter. "Besides the belief that one changes people first, these power-equalization approaches also place major emphasis on other aspects of the human phenomena of organizations. They are, for example, centrally concerned with affect; with morale, sensitivity, psychological security. Secondly, they value evolutionary, internally generated change in individuals, groups, and organizations over externally planned or implemented change. Thirdly, they place much value on human growth and fulfillment as well as upon task accomplishment; and they often have stretched the degree of causal connection between the two. Finally, . . . the power-equalization approaches . . . shared a normative belief that power in organizations should be more equally distributed than in most existent 'authoritarian' hierarchies," he writes.

The PE approaches are further described with reference to goals; communication; group pressure, group cohesiveness, and conformity; and decision making.

Power-equalization practices are most applicable in situations requiring creativity and flexibility rather than in highly programmed task areas.

Topics

Change Goals	Group Processes
Change Strategy	Manipulation
Cohesion	Power Equalization
Communications	Scanlon Plan
Conformity	Self-Change
Consensus	Structural Change
Creativity	Technological Change
Decision Making	T-Group
Flexibility	

Section 2

DEVELOPMENT STRATEGIES AND TECHNIQUES

Organization development is an action field. This becomes especially evident when one examines the amount of literature devoted to descriptions of various change strategies and techniques. It is possible to generate lists of different types of OD techniques without ever gaining a feeling that all the possibilities have been exhausted. For the purposes of this section we have limited greatly the number of subsections describing these activities. The eighteen subsections included in this section exemplify the range and the nature of such activities.

Some of these subsections include many references while others have only one or two. This represents both the popularity and time of development of these activities. The laboratory training approach has a longer history and has witnessed far greater interest (especially in the 1960s) than many other approaches. In fact, many individuals trace the origins of OD to laboratory training itself. Other approaches are recent innovations and, as of yet, have received less attention and utilization.

Ideally, we would also be able to provide a number of works which compare and contrast OD strategies and techniques to reveal the relative effectiveness of each. Unfortunately, only one empirically based study of this nature has been reported to date. The section begins with this investigation by Bowers (1973), which provides a comparison across four major types of activities.

Bowers, David G. "OD Techniques and Their Results in 23 Organizations: The Michigan ICL Study." JOURNAL OF APPLIED BEHAVIORAL SCIENCE 9, no. 1 (1973): 21-43.

This article analyzes in terms of OD the data collected by use of the Survey of Organizations questionnaire from more than 14,000 respondents in twenty-three organizations which participated in the Inter-company Longitudinal Study. It compares four experimental treatments (Survey Feedback, Inter-Personal Process Consultation, Task Process Consultation, and Laboratory Training) with two control treatments (Data Handback and No Treatment) to determine their comparative associations with improved organizational functioning as measured by the questionnaire.

"The results indicate that Survey Feedback was associated with statistically significant improvement on a majority of measures, that Interpersonal Process Consultation was associated with improvement on a minority of measures, that Task Process Consultation was associated with declines. In addition, organizational climate emerges as a potentially extremely important conditioner of these results, with Survey Feedback appearing as the only treatment associated with substantial improvement in the variables of this domain."

Topics

Change Processes
Change Strategy
Change Technology
Climate
Laboratory Training

Organizational Climate
Process Consultation
Survey Feedback
Survey of Organizations
Work Group

BEHAVIOR MODIFICATION

Luthans, Fred, and Kreitner, Robert. ORGANIZATIONAL BEHAVIOR MODIFICATION. Glenview, Ill.: Scott, Foresman and Co., 1975. 214 p.

This book focuses on operant learning theory and the principles of behavior modification as a means of achieving better understanding, prediction, and control of organizational behavior. Included in this ten-chapter volume are learning theory, behavior modification, the identification and use of behavioral events, a problem-solving model of behavioral contingency management, reinforcement and punishment in behavior control, shaping intervention strategies, case illustrations, ethical implications, and preconditions for developing the organizational behavior modification approach to change.

Contents

1. A New Perspective
2. Learning Theory Background
3. Principles of Behavior Modification
4. Behavioral Contingency Management
5. Positive Control
6. Negative Control
7. Shaping, Modeling, and Self-Control
8. Organizational Behavior Modification: Some Actual Cases
9. Analyzing Ethical Issues
10. Preconditions for Future Development

Topics

Behavioral Contingency
  Management
Behavior Change
Behavior Modification

Change Agent
Change Strategy
Climate
Communications

Ethics
Expectancy Theory
Feedback
Organizational Behavior
Modification

Performance
Punishment
Reinforcement
Rewards
Training

CONFRONTATION AND CONFLICT RESOLUTION

Beckhard, Richard. "The Confrontation Meeting." HARVARD BUSINESS RE-
VIEW 45, no. 2 (1967): 149-54.

Beckhard describes a technique developed to involve all levels of
an organization in getting a rapid reading of its own health and
setting action plans for improving it.

He believes that the method is appropriate where the following
conditions exist: "There is a need for the total management group
to examine its own workings. Very limited time is available for
the activity. Top management wishes to improve conditions quickly.
There is enough cohesion in the top team to ensure follow-up.
There is real commitment to resolving the issues on the part of
top management. The organization is experiencing, or has recently
experienced, some major change."

The technique includes climate setting, information collecting, information sharing, priority setting and group action planning, organization action planning, immediate followup by top team, and
progress review.

Topics

Change Strategy
Climate
Commitment

Confrontation Meeting
Diagnosis/Evaluation

Blake, Robert R.; Mouton, Jane S.; and Sloma, Richard [L.]. "The Union-
Management Intergroup Laboratory: Strategy for Resolving Intergroup Conflict."
JOURNAL OF APPLIED BEHAVIORAL SCIENCE 1, no. 1 (1965): 25-57.

An account of an intergroup laboratory is presented with eight
major phases identified and described: orientation; intragroup development of own image and its image of the other; exchange of
images across groups; clarification of images; intragroup diagnosis
of present relationship, exchange of diagnosis across groups; con-
solidation of key issues and sources of friction; and planning next
steps.

The authors point out that long term conflicts are difficult to resolve. The real test of such a laboratory is "when new issues and
different problems arise in the relationship."

Topics

Conflict/Conflict Resolution

Merger. Laboratory

Blake, Robert R.; Shepard, Herbert A.; and Mouton, Jane S. MANAGING INTERGROUP CONFLICT IN INDUSTRY. Houston: Gulf Publishing Co., 1964. xiii, 210 p.

The thesis of this book is that conflict resolved through problem-solving methods can lead to creative and innovative thinking. A framework for understanding intergroup disagreement is presented. The authors suggest nine possible solutions to conflict on the basis of the importance of the outcome. The outcomes include win-lose power struggle, third-party judgment, fate, withdrawal, isolation, indifference or ignorance, peaceful coexistence, splitting the difference, and problem solving. Each solution is evaluated.

Problem solving is suggested as the most constructive of the solutions. "Intergroup problem-solving emphasizes solving the problems, not accommodating different points of view. This problem-solving approach identifies the causes of reservation, doubt and misunderstandings between groups confronted with disagreement. Alternative ways of approaching conflict resolution are explored. In true problem-solving, the alternative solutions which emerge may not be ones held by either of the contending groups at the onset," the authors conclude.

Contents

1. Foundations and dynamics of intergroup behavior
2. The win-lose orientation to intergroup disagreement
3. Win-lose power struggles in industrial life
4. Using third-party judgment to resolve intergroup disputes
5. Fate
6. Withdrawal, isolation, and indifference in intergroup relations
7. Peaceful coexistence as a condition of agreement
8. Compromise, bargaining and other forms of splitting the difference
9. Problem-solving: A third approach to agreement
10. Intervention into situations of intergroup conflict
11. Strategies for improving headquarters-field relations
12. Problem-solving interventions in setting of labor-management conflict
13. An intergroup problem-solving approach to mergers

Topics

Change Strategy   Problem Solving
Conflict/Conflict Resolution   Third Party

Golembiewski, Robert T., and Blumberg, Arthur. "Confrontation as a Training Design in Complex Organizations." JOURNAL OF APPLIED BEHAVIORAL SCIENCE 3, no. 4 (1967): 525-47.

A three-day confrontation experience was used as part of a week-long workshop which was, in turn, part of a long-range management and organizational development effort. Three-D images ("How we see ourselves; How we see the other group; How we think the other group sees us") were generated by functionally related departments, including several hierarchical levels.

The results included positive attitudinal changes toward members of other work groups.

The authors note that, "the experience supports the claim that relatively short time-periods spent in a confrontation design can prove useful in handling substantial unfinished business and in freeing-up relations among individuals in complex organizations. In sum, a non-T-group technique can generate much learning commonly associated with that technique."

Topics

Attitude/Attitude Change	Management Training
Confrontation	Development
	T-Group

Lewicki, Roy J., and Alderfer, Clayton P. "The Tensions between Research and Intervention in Intergroup Conflict." JOURNAL OF APPLIED BEHAVIORAL SCIENCE 9, no. 4 (1973): 424-49.

A chronological presentation of an intervention by behavioral scientists in a labor/management conflict provides the basis for discussing major issues of concern in intervention in intergroup conflict. Two suggestions are offered to help avoid potential difficulties: (1) "if a third party is contacted by one of the groups in conflict, he should make contact as quickly as possible with the other party"; (2) "the combined researcher-interventionist may have to sacrifice his research goals for short-run gain" (p. 449).

This article is followed in the same journal issue by critical comments from Bert R. Brown, "Reflections on Missing the Broad Side of a Barn," pp. 450-58, and Frank Friedlander, "The Innocence of Research," pp. 459-63, as well as a rejoinder from the article's authors, pp. 463-68.

Topics

Action Research	Consultation
Change Strategy	Intervention
Conflict/Conflict Resolution	Union

Walton, Richard E. INTERPERSONAL PEACEMAKING: CONFRONTATIONS AND THIRD PARTY INTERVENTIONS. Reading, Mass.: Addison-Wesley, 1969. viii, 151 p.

Walton describes the role of a third party who helps members of an organization manage interpersonal conflict.

Three case studies provide the basis for a series of generalizations regarding frameworks, activities, and attributes of the third-party consultant.

Contents

1. Introduction
2. Bill--Lloyd: Negotiating a relationship
3. Mack--Sy: Confronting a deeply felt conflict
4. Fred--Charles: Searching for an accommodation
5. Diagnostic model of interpersonal conflict
6. Confrontations and strategic third-party functions
7. Third-party interventions and tactical choices
8. Third-party attributes
9. Summary and conclusions

Topics

Change Agent
Conflict/Conflict Resolution
Confrontation
Consultation
Diagnosis/Evaluation
Innovation

Interpersonal Processes
Motivation
Norms
Risk/Risk-Taking
Role
Third Party

DATA FEEDBACK

Alper, S. William, and Klein, Stuart M. "Feedback following Opinion Surveys." PERSONNEL ADMINISTRATION, November-December 1970, pp. 104-6.

This article focuses on the effects, as revealed in attitude surveys, of various approaches to providing feedback or not providing feedback to employees. Employee perceptions of constructive utilization of survey results was maximized where feedback occurred and minimized under the "no feedback" condition. The most preferred feedback procedure was in departmental or project meetings (70 percent favorable), followed by larger group meetings (57 percent), and written form (39 percent). Further, employees strongly favored feedback procedures where problems were discussed to those meetings where significant problems were not discussed.

The authors suggest from these results that the lack of feedback tends to frustrate employees and that discussion of problems, rather than producing lower morale, increases the belief that management is going to use the survey effectively.

Topics

Attitude/Attitude Change
Feedback

Survey Feedback

Anderson, John [W.]. "Giving and Receiving Feedback." In ORGANIZATIONAL CHANGE AND DEVELOPMENT, edited by Gene W. Dalton, Paul R. Lawrence, and Larry E. Greiner, pp. 339-46. Homewood, Ill.: Irwin-Dorsey, 1970.

Suggestions are presented for the use of feedback in a team laboratory. The following conditions maximize the usefulness of feedback: an intent of helpfulness should be present; it should be given directly in an atmosphere of mutual trust; descriptive information should be given instead of evaluative feedback; feedback should be specific and supported by clear and recent examples; it should be given when the receiver is ready to accept it; it should be checked with others to insure its validity; it should include only things over which the receiver has some power to change; and it should be limited by what the person receiving the feedback can handle at any given time.

When receiving feedback, one should try not to be defensive; try to find relevant examples to clarify the point; be sure one understands by summarizing what has been said; explore feelings about the feedback; and reserve the right to evaluate and act upon the feedback.

Topics

Defensiveness
Feedback

Team Development Laboratory
Trust

Aplin, John C., Jr., and Thompson, Duane E. "Feedback: Key to Survey-Based Change." PUBLIC PERSONNEL MANAGEMENT, November-December 1974, pp. 524-30.

Feedback activities are presented as keys to the effective utilization of survey data. According to these authors, both content and process objectives must be emphasized if feedback is to result in positive outcomes.

Six phases of feedback activities are identified: contracting, validity testing, problem identification and analysis, problem solving, closure, and followup.

Topics

Change Strategy
Change Technology
Content
Feedback
Laboratory Training

Problem Solving
Process
Process Consultation
Survey Feedback

Baumgartel, Howard. "Using Employee Questionnaire Results for Improving Organizations: The Survey 'Feedback' Experiment." KANSAS BUSINESS REVIEW 12, no. 12 (1959): 2-6.

The early survey feedback experiments conducted in the Detroit Edison Company by the Institute for Social Research's Survey Research Center are described briefly. Questionnaire responses indicated positive change resulted from the survey feedback process. The author discusses reasons for the success of this approach and conditions necessary for its beneficial application.

Topics

Survey Feedback

Bowers, David G., and Franklin, Jerome L. "Basic Concepts of Survey Feedback." In THE 1974 ANNUAL HANDBOOK FOR GROUP FACILITATORS, edited by J.W. Pfeiffer and J.E. Jones, pp. 221-25. LaJolla, Calif.: University Associates Publishers, 1974.

> Survey feedback is described as "a relatively complex guidance method which draws upon the device of the questionnaire survey to upgrade and make more complete, rational, and adequate a process inherent in social organizations."

> The authors distinguish between survey feedback as a process and the meaning of data used in the process. Three critical aspects of the data are identified as the accuracy of the picture yielded, the clarity of questionnaire items, and the perceived threat. Critical aspects of survey feedback as a process include the resource person's role, relationships among group members, and sequencing of feedback through an organization.

Topics

Change Agent	Survey Feedback
Group Development	Threat

French, John R.P., Jr.; Sherwood, John; and Bradford, David L. "Change in Self-Identity in a Management Training Conference." JOURNAL OF APPLIED BEHAVIORAL SCIENCE 2, no. 2 (1966): 210-18.

> Two two-week human relations training conferences were used to test hypotheses about the effects of feedback on self-identity. "The amount of feedback (communicated objective public identity--COPI) was systematically varied and was related to responses on questionnaires asking about self-perception," the authors contend.

> Information collected at the beginning, halfway point, end point, and ten months after the end supported the propositions that a person's self-identity is influenced by the opinions others have of him which they communicate to him and that the more information which is communicated, the more change there is in self-identity. The state of the individual also is important; the more he is dissatisfied with his present self-perceptions, the more likely he is to change them.

Topics

Feedback	Self-Concept
Human Relations Training	T-Group

Hand, Herbert H.; Estafen, Bernard D.; Sims, Henry P., Jr. "How Effective is Data Survey and Feedback as a Technique of Organization Development? An Experiment." JOURNAL OF APPLIED BEHAVIORAL SCIENCE 11, no. 3 (1975): 333-47.

> A business simulation game served as the context for evaluating affective and performance changes attributed to an OD intervention.

Members of both the seventeen experimental teams (e.g., those receiving the intervention) and the nineteen control teams (no intervention) were business students, and the consultants were doctoral students enrolled in an OD course. The OD treatment (Data Survey and Feedback) allowed information analysis and member intercommunication, with the focus on developing the team's decision-making efficiency and effectiveness.

Need satisfaction was increased for three of five scales (social, esteem, self-realization), for the experimental group over the level of the control group. Two scales (security, autonomy) revealed differences in the predicted direction but of a nonsignificant magnitude. Neither of the two performance variables (sales forecast error, return on investment) were significantly affected by the OD intervention.

The discussion stresses the importance of the criteria and adequacy of time span for capturing changes in performance measures.

Topics

Autonomy	Feedback
Change Strategy	Gaming
Communications	Performance
Consultant	Satisfaction
Decision Making	

Klein, Stuart M.; Kraut, Allen I.; and Wolfson, Alan [D.]. "Employee Reactions to Attitude Survey Feedback: A Study of the Impact of Structure and Process." ADMINISTRATIVE SCIENCE QUARTERLY 16, no. 4 (1971): 497-514.

"This study examines the impact of attitude survey feedback on recipients' attitudes toward the feedback process and their perceptions of survey utilization. Two populations were examined in a natural experimental setting: manufacturing employees and manufacturing managers. Independent variables were of two classes: structure and process. It was hypothesized that each class would be positively associated with the dependent variables. In the main, however, the process variables were more powerful predictors of the dependent measures. Analysis disclosed that structure facilitates process and is its natural antecedent. A model of information dissemination was posited whereby the relationship between structural variables and attitudes was moderated by process variables. This was supported by the data. In addition it was found that the process variables were of two classes: communication and involvement, the former predicting better to satisfaction with survey feedback and the latter predicting better to perceived utilization of the survey's results. Finally, it was found that the management group perceived utilization and satisfaction as highly related, probably because of the decision-making orientation of this group."

Topics

Attitude/Attitude Change	Satisfaction
Communication	Structure
Decision Making	Survey Feedback
Process	

Mann, Floyd C. "Studying and Creating Change: A Means to Understanding Social Organization." RESEARCH ON INDUSTRIAL HUMAN RELATIONS. Industrial Relations Research Association, Publication no. 17. New York: Harper, 1957.

The author outlines the survey feedback process. Classroom learning is compared to the feedback process on the dimensions of objectives, setting, informational content, method, who the trainees are, training unit, who the change agent is, how the pace is set, length of the process, amount of tension, assumptions about attitudes, and measurement of effectiveness.

Topics

Attitude/Attitude Change	Learning
Change Agent	Survey Feedback

Miles, Matthew B., et al. "Data Feedback and Organizational Change in a School System." In SENSITIVITY TRAINING AND THE LABORATORY APPROACH, edited by Robert T. Golembiewski and Arthur Blumberg, pp. 352-61. Itasca, Ill.: F.E. Peacock, 1970.

This article provides a good description of the use of data feedback in an organizational change program. It defines survey feedback as "a process in which outside staff and members of the organization collaboratively gather, analyze and interpret data that deal with various aspects of the organization's functioning and its members' work lives, and using the data as a base, begin to correctively alter the organizational structure and the members' work relationships."

The various components (presentation of data, meetings, analysis of process) of survey feedback are described, as are their possible effects. The authors note that the data may cause any one or combination of the following to occur: confirmation of previously held feelings, contradiction of beliefs, and/or encouragement of an inquiry about why people responded as they did to the survey.

Topics

Diagnosis/Evaluation	Group Processes
Feedback	Survey Feedback

Nadler, David A.; Mirvis, Phillip H.; and Cammann, Cortlandt. "The Ongoing Feedback System: Experimenting with a New Managerial Tool." ORGANIZATIONAL DYNAMICS, Spring 1976, pp. 63-80.

An examination of feedback systems in organizations reveals five common major weaknesses. An experiment is described which attempts to establish an ongoing feedback system minimizing such weaknesses. The experiment included experimental and control branches in a midwestern bank. Results indicate differential degrees of implementation of the system and "that improvements in attitudes and performance are seen in the branches where the system was used effectively, relatively little change is observed in the control branches, and decreases in attitudes and performance occur in the branches where the system was used ineffectively or not used at all."

Topics

Attitude/Attitude Change   Feedback
Change Strategy   Performance

Neff, Frank[lin W.]. "Survey Research: A Tool for Problem Diagnosis and Improvement in Organizations." In APPLIED SOCIOLOGY, edited by S. Miller and A. Gouldner, pp. 23-38. New York: Free Press, 1965.

Neff considers the use of survey feedback in organizational improvement efforts. Neff has based this work on the experiences of Floyd Mann and other researchers from the Institute for Social Research at the University of Michigan.

The author emphasizes the desired involvement of organizational members as well as researchers in the survey feedback process. According to him, it is important that organizational members have a good understanding of the questions in the instrument and that they are active in making the diagnosis.

Topics

Diagnosis/Evaluation   Problem Solving
Involvement   Survey Feedback

FLEXI-TIME

Golembiewski, Robert T.; Hilles, Rick; and Kagno, Munro S. "A Longitudinal Study of Flexi-time Effects: Some Consequences of an OD Structural Intervention." JOURNAL OF APPLIED BEHAVIORAL SCIENCE 10, no. 4 (1974): 503-32.

The authors describe the implementation, functioning, and results of change involving more flexible working hours in R&D settings. The change consisted of allowing each employee to work different hours during different days to accumulate the necessary time for a 35-hour work week. Attitudinal and "hard data" (e.g., absenteeism, cost of support services, sick days) were compared between two experimental units and one control unit. Responses from managerial personnel were solicited about roles as supervisors and subordinates. Data collection points included one pre-test, one short post-test, and a long post-test. The results of this flexi-time program were generally positive, as predicted.

The authors caution that it is difficult to tell how much of the impact resulted from the intervention and how much was attributable to the culture of the organization.

Topics

Absence	Flexi-Time
Attendance	Structural Change
Change Strategy	Values
Culture	

JOB DESIGN

Alderfer, Clayton P. "Job Enlargement and the Organizational Context." PERSONNEL PSYCHOLOGY 22, no. 4 (1969): 418-26.

This analysis of a job enlargement program in a manufacturing organization stresses the possibility that mixed results may occur. Specifically, Alderfer indicates that since such change occurs within settings involving other people, considerable attention should be given to the interpersonal consequences of changes.

Topics

Attitude/Attitude Change	Satisfaction
Job Enlargement	

_____. "The Organizational Syndrome." ADMINISTRATIVE SCIENCE QUARTERLY 12 (1967): 440-60.

This study in one organization stressed the effects of job enlargement on satisfaction. The major findings were that satisfaction with respect from supervisors decreased as job complexity increased and as seniority increased. Secondly, satisfaction with use of skills and abilities increased as job complexity increased. Two explanations for the breakdown in superior-to-subordinate relationships are suggested. The first is that more complex jobs required levels of interpersonal competence not reached in the organization studied. The second explanation is that rapid growth and technological change resulted in career anxiety which put strains on the superior-to-subordinate relationship.

Topics

Job Enlargement	Superior-Subordinate
Organization Growth	Relationship
Satisfaction	Technological Change

Anderson, John W. "The Impact of Technology on Job Enrichment." PERSONNEL 47 (September-October 1970): 29-37.

Job enrichment is discussed in the context of organizations relying on four different technologies--service, heavy assembly, electronics, and processing. Both the form of job enrichment and the problems associated with it vary with the technology. Variance is particularly evident in the ability to influence major elements described as essential to affecting motivation.

Topics

Job Enrichment   Technology
Motivation

Donaldson, Lex. "Job Enlargement: A Multidimensional Process." HUMAN RELATIONS 28, no. 7 (1975): 593-610.

This article describes a job enlargement experiment with female assemblers of electric domestic appliances in Scotland. An experimental and a roughly equivalent comparison group were used to evaluate the effects of changes on attitudes. Expected increases were achieved in satisfaction associated with greater work variety, novelty, and felt use of abilities. There was, however, some dissatisfaction resulting from decreased social interaction and increased work load.

Topics

Attitude/Attitude Change   Job Enlargement
Change Strategy   Role
Horizontal Job Loading   Satisfaction
Job Design   Vertical Job Loading

Ford, Robert N. MOTIVATION THROUGH THE WORK ITSELF. New York: American Management Association, 1969. 267 p.

Ford summarizes attempts of American Telephone and Telegraph to reduce employee turnover through job enrichment. Included are examinations of the job enrichment efforts, results of these efforts, and general theory concerning the effects of job design on motivation.

Contents

1. Introduction
2. Studies in AT & T's Treasury Department
    Part A--A New Approach to Job Motivation: Improving the Work Itself, Robert N. Ford and Malcolm B. Gillette
    Part B--Permanency of Results: Treasury Revisited 18 Months Later
3. Results of the Controlled Experiments
4. A Critical Visit to a Work-Itself Site
5. Insights from the Studies
6. Some Questions and Answers About the Work-Itself Approach
7. The Art of Reshaping Jobs
8. Following Through to an Improved Job
9. An Overview of the Work-Itself idea

Appendix A--Treasury Department Manpower Utilization, Malcolm
    B. Gillette
Appendix B--The Framemen Trial, Harry J. Sheaffer

Topics

Durability of Change   Job Enrichment
Feedback   Motivation
Job Design   Turnover

Frank, Linda L., and Hackman, J. Richard. "A Failure of Job Enrichment:
The Case of the Change that Wasn't." JOURNAL OF APPLIED BEHAVIORAL
SCIENCE 11, no. 4 (1975): 413-36.

The failure to increase job satisfaction, raise motivation, and improve performance through a job enrichment program in one department of a bank is attributed to several factors including a lack of
attention to workgroup theory and the fact that the intervention
did not affect the work itself. Four guides are offered for success
in organizational change projects, suggesting the need for a theoretical base, an explicit diagnosis, the preparation of contingency
plans to deal with unanticipated problems and opportunities, and
continuous evaluation as the basis for adjusting actions.

Topics

Autonomy   Job Design
Change Strategy   Job Enrichment
Commitment   Motivation
Consultation   Motivation Potential Score
Diagnosis/Evaluation   Skill Variety
Feedback   Task Identity
Group Process   Task Significance
Identity

Hackman, J. Richard, and Lawler, Edward E. III. "Employee Reactions to Job
Characteristics." JOURNAL OF APPLIED PSYCHOLOGY 55, no. 3 (1971):
259-86.

Work conditions were measured on a conceptual framework to determine those conditions which promoted internal motivation. The
test group was composed of 208 employees of a telephone company
who worked on thirteen different jobs. The significant independent
variables were: "(a) a measure of strength of desire for the satisfaction of 'higher order' needs (e.g., obtaining feelings of accomplishment, personal growth); and (b) descriptions of jobs on four
core dimensions (variety, autonomy, task identity, feedback)."

The prediction was borne out that when jobs are high on the four
core dimensions, employees who have a strong desire for higher
order need satisfaction tend to have high motivation, high job
satisfaction, low absenteeism rates, and favorable performance reviews.

The authors concluded that " . . . results of the present research suggest that the substantial motivational potential of jobs can be realized only when the psychological demands and opportunities of jobs mesh well with the personal needs and goals of employees who work on them."

(See also Lawler, Edward E. III; Hackman, J. Richard; and Kaufman, Stanley, below.)

Topics

Autonomy   Motivation
Feedback   Performance
Job Enlargement   Satisfaction

Hackman, J. Richard, et al. "A New Strategy for Job Enrichment." CALIFORNIA MANAGEMENT REVIEW 17, no. 4 (1975): 57-71.

A strategy is provided for evaluating jobs to determine if job enrichment is appropriate, and, if so, which specific actions will maximize chances for success. The diagnostic procedures are designed to evaluate the objective characteristics of jobs; levels of motivation, satisfaction, and performance; and levels of growth need strength.

Five types of action are suggested as a means of improving work experiences and productivity: (1) forming natural work units; (2) combining tasks; (3) establishing client relationships; (4) vertical loading; and (5) opening feedback channels.

The authors present results from an experience in the Travelers Insurance Companies to indicate the types and degrees of benefits which have been realized from the implementation of such procedures.

Topics

Autonomy   Job Diagnostic Survey
Behavior Change   Job Enrichment
Change Strategy   Motivation
Diagnosis/Evaluation   Performance
Feedback   Vertical Job Loading
Job Design

Herzberg, Frederick. "One More Time: How Do You Motivate Employees?" HARVARD BUSINESS REVIEW 46, no. 1 (1968): 53-62.

The author states his basic ideas regarding motivators and hygiene factors. The hygiene factors include supervision, work conditions, salary status, personal life, relationships with subordinates, relationships with supervisors, relationships with peers, and company policy and administration. Motivators include recognition, achievement, the work itself, responsibility, advancement, and growth.

"The only way to motivate the employee is to give him challenging work in which he can assume responsibility," Herzberg argues.

Topics

Horizontal Job Loading	Motivation
Hygiene Factor	Vertical Job Loading
Job Enrichment	

Hulin, Charles L., and Blood, Milton R. "Job Enlargement, Individual Differences, and Worker Responses." PSYCHOLOGICAL BULLETIN 69, no. 1 (1968): 41-55.

Positive effects resulting from job enlargement are questioned on the basis of a review of studies. The authors cite evidence to suggest that some common assumptions embraced by proponents of job enlargement are of questionable validity. Of special note is evidence indicating that some workers prefer routine, repetition, and specified work methods to change, variety, and decision making. The authors suggest "the general conclusion regarding the effects of job enlargement on job satisfaction and/or motivation is overstated and may be applicable to only certain segments of the working population" (p. 48). This segment is defined as white-collar and supervisory workers and nonalienated blue-collar workers. These writers develop a model describing the relationship between job size and satisfaction as moderated by alienation from middle-class work-related values. They argue that "this model adequately accounts for most of the problems and contradictions which exist in the literature" (p. 41).

Topics

Alienation	Motivation
Job Enlargement	Satisfaction

Kahn, Robert L. "The Work Module--A Tonic for Lunchpail Lassitude." PSYCHOLOGY TODAY 6, no. 9 (1973): 94-95.

The establishment of work modules ("a time-task unit--the smallest allocation of time that is economically and psychologically meaningful") is suggested as a means of humanizing work. Humanized work, the author says, "(1) should not damage, degrade, humiliate, exhaust, or persistently bore the worker; (2) should be interesting and satisfying; (3) should utilize many of the valued skills the worker already has, and provide opportunity to acquire others; (4) should enhance, or at least leave unimpaired, the worker's ability to perform other life roles--as spouse, parent, citizen, and friend, for example; (5) should pay a wage sufficient to enable the worker to live a comfortable life."

According to the author, a system of work modules would increase worker satisfaction, "self-utilization (use of one's skills and abilities) and self-development (acquisition of new skills and abilities)."

He views the system as improving the fit between the individual and his job.

Costs and other organizational constraints associated with the implementation of a work module system are also discussed.

Topics

Absence	Satisfaction
Autonomy	Turnover
Job Enrichment	Work Module

Lawler, Edward E. III. "Job Design and Employee Motivation." PERSONNEL PSYCHOLOGY 22 (1969): 426-34.

Lawler argues that "when a job is structured in a way that makes intrinsic rewards appear to result from good performance, then the job itself can be a very effective motivator. In addition . . . if job content is to be a source of motivation, the job must allow for meaningful feedback, test the individual's valued abilities, and allow a great amount of self-control by the job holder. In order for this to happen, jobs must be enlarged on both the vertical and horizontal dimensions. Further . . . job enlargement is more likely to lead to increased product quality than to increased productivity. A review of the literature on job enlargement generally tended to confirm these predictions" (p. 434).

Topics

Expectancy Theory	Job Rotation
Horizontal Job Loading	Motivation
Job Design	Scanlon Plan
Job Enlargement	Vertical Job Loading

Lawler, Edward E. III; Hackman, J. Richard; and Kaufman, Stanley. "Effects of Job Redesign: A Field Experiment." JOURNAL OF APPLIED SOCIAL PSY-CHOLOGY 3, no. 1 (1973): 49-62.

Thirty-nine female employees of a telephone company participated in a job enrichment program. Changes were made which increased variety and decision making on the job. However, no change in work motivation, job involvement, or growth need satisfaction resulted from the changes; instead, the changes had a significant negative impact on interpersonal relationships. Older employees reported less satisfaction with the quality of their interpersonal relationships, and supervisors whose jobs were affected by the changes reported less job security and reduced interpersonal satisfaction.

The data reported suggest "any positive motivational effects that might have accrued as a result of the increases in variety and autonomy in the directory assistance job were more than counteracted by the negative effects the changes had on the attitudes and behavior of the [service assistants]." A suggested reason for the negative reactions is the lack of participation by those involved in planning the job redesign.

(See also Hackman, J. Richard, and Lawler, Edward E. III, above.)

Topics

Autonomy   Participation
Job Enrichment   Satisfaction
Motivation

Paul, William J., Jr.; Robertson, Keith B.; and Herzberg, Frederick. "Job Enrichment Pays Off." HARVARD BUSINESS REVIEW 47, no. 2 (1969): 61-78.

A summary is presented of five studies on job enrichment. Using a variety of criteria to fit the various participants, the authors conclude that job enrichment programs enhance job performance (but not necessarily job satisfaction) in a variety of settings. They theorize that satisfaction is a result of performance and, therefore, may change more slowly.

Topics

Job Enrichment   Satisfaction
Performance

Sirota, David, and Wolfson, Alan D. "Job Enrichment: What are the Obstacles?" PERSONNEL, May-June, 1972, pp. 8-17.

Eleven categories of obstacles inhibiting the implementation of job enrichment are discussed. These include educational (not knowing what to do); ideological (a belief in the superiority of job fragmentation); organizational (costs, changing roles, functional splits); managerial (resistance to change); technological (constraints concerning major investments); the employee (lack of desire or skill to do enriched jobs); the enricher (implementation strategies); diagnosis (the lack thereof); "Prove it here" (emphasis on uniqueness of organizations); "Nothing new here" (old ideas restated); and time (requirements for successful implementation).

Topics

Change Strategy   Resistance to Change
Job Enrichment

Stewart, Paul A., Jr. JOB ENLARGEMENT. . . IN THE SHOP . . . IN THE MANAGEMENT FUNCTION. Iowa City: Center for Labor and Management, College of Business Administration, University of Iowa, 1967. 64 p.

This monograph is a study of the Maytag Company's experiences with job enlargement in blue-collar and managerial positions.

Contents

Chapter I Introduction

Chapter II Job Enlargement in the Shop
   Preparing for Job Enlargement
   Job Enlargement Experience
   Advantages and Limitations
   Summary Statement
Chapter III Job Enlargement through Management Design
   Purpose, Objectives and Principles
   Purpose and Scope of Positions
   Definitions and Information Requirements
   Group Activities and the Task Force
   Summary Statement

Topics

Change Strategy   Job Enlargement

Zeitlin, Lawrence R. "A Little Larceny Can Do a Lot for Employee Morale." PSYCHOLOGY TODAY 5, no. 1 (1971): 22, 24, 26, 64.

The author advocates controlled stealing as a form of job enrichment.

Topics

Job Enrichment   Morale

LABORATORY TRAINING, ENCOUNTER GROUP, HUMAN RELATIONS TRAINING, SENSITIVITY TRAINING, AND T-GROUP

Argyris, Chris A. "On the Future of Laboratory Education." JOURNAL OF APPLIED BEHAVIORAL SCIENCE 3, no. 2 (1967): 153-87.

Issues of learning are discussed, with special emphasis on the laboratory approach. Argyris distinguishes the laboratory approach from more traditional approaches by its stress on feelings, group maintenance, and student control. Argyris argues, however, that feelings are valuable only when valid and not as ends in themselves. The validity of feelings is established through multiple perceptions by different individuals.

The artificiality of the situation is a danger of the laboratory approach. "Learning that is laboratory-bound is of interest, but it can be dangerous because the individual could leave, feeling that the only world that is a good one is the one in the laboratory." This feeling would not motivate the individual to increase his interpersonal competence in the real world.

Additional comments relate to learning in situations where psychological success, confirmation, and essentiality are maximized or minimized; the value of here-and-now data; and the motives and needs of those attracted to laboratory education.

Topics

Feelings   Laboratory Training
Here-and-Now Data   Motivation
Interpersonal Competence   Transfer of Training

_____. "T-groups for Organizational Effectiveness." HARVARD BUSINESS REVIEW 42, no. 2 (1964): 60-74.

A rationale is presented for the use of T-groups as a means of improving organizational effectiveness. Basically, this method provides a supportive situation in which one is able to experience the ineffectiveness of old values and increase his abilities to use new values. The method is seen as effective because the method of teaching is congruent with the values being taught.

According to Argyris, a change cannot really be effective and permanent until the new values are accepted throughout the organization. In addition, he notes that the results of laboratory education are "individualistic"; they are a result of a particular individual in a particular organization.

Topics

Laboratory Training   T-Group
Organization Effectiveness

Bass, Bernard M. "The Anarchist Movement and the T-groups." JOURNAL OF APPLIED BEHAVIORAL SCIENCE 3, no. 2 (1967): 211-26.

Bass offers cautions regarding the use of T-groups in organizational development. Of special concern is that more mature individuals may make less effective organizations. The emphasis on freedom in T-groups does not seem to be matched by an equally necessary emphasis on individual responsibility.

A second major issue is the transfer of diagnostic skills and self-awareness to the organizational setting. According to Bass, participants must be taught to transfer if that process is to be effective. He suggests eight approaches (with examples) for increasing the transfer of T-group training. He believes that T-grouping without supplementary activities is not sufficient for organizational development.

Topics

Diagnosis/Evaluation   T-Group
Self-Awareness   Transfer of Training

Bennis, Warren G., and Schein, Edgar H. "Principles and Strategies in the Use of Laboratory Training for Improving Social Systems." In THE PLANNING OF CHANGE, edited by Warren G. Bennis, Kenneth D. Benne, and Robert Chin, pp. 335-57. New York: Holt, Rinehart and Winston, 1969.

This is an excerpt from a book previously published by the authors (Schein and Bennis, p. 114). The article reiterates much of what Bennis has previously stated about the goals of change activities and conditions appropriate for implementing planned social change.

Topics

Change Agent   Change Strategy
Change Goals   Laboratory Training

Bolman, Lee. "Laboratory Versus Lecture in Training Executives." JOURNAL OF APPLIED BEHAVIORAL SCIENCE 6, no. 3 (1970): 323-35.

The study involved four groups of business executives participating in a six-week program designed to increase their competence in dealing with interpersonal phenomena. For members of two control groups one week of the program consisted of lectures, discussions, and readings on human relations. Members of two experimental groups instead participated in T-group sessions.

Each participant completed the Analysis of Personal Behavior in Groups questionnaire three times: before arrival, after the one-week session, and at the completion of this six-week program. Tapes of discussions were also gathered at three different times: during the human relations (one-week) program, at the end of the program, and during the end of the six-week program. The questionnaire responses together with behavior scores taken from the tapes were used to judge changes.

The author concluded: "Both types of programs produced equal change in participants' stated beliefs about effective interpersonal behavior. Laboratory training showed greater effects on participants' perceptions of themselves and on their behavior as analyzed from tape recordings of case discussion meetings. However, there was evidence that the participants had difficulty transferring learning from the T-Group to other parts of the program and that there was considerable fade-out of the effects of the training."

Topics

Analysis of Personal Behavior   Sensitivity Training
  in Groups Questionnaire   Team Building/Development
Change Agent   Team Development Laboratory
Change Processes   T-Group
Consultant   Therapy
Diagnosis/Evaluation   Transfer of Training
Process Consultation

Bradford, Leland P., and Mial, D.J. "Human Relations Laboratory Training." In TRAINING AND DEVELOPMENT HANDBOOK, edited by Robert L. Craig and Lester R. Billel, pp. 251-66. New York: McGraw-Hill, 1967.

The authors provide a rationale for the use of laboratory training as a means of achieving necessary aspects of management development. Laboratory training is said to meet the following conditions of learning: exposure of behavior, feedback, atmosphere, knowledge as a map, experimentation and practice, application, and learning how to learn.

Topics

Feedback
Human Relations Training
Laboratory Training

Learning
Management Training/
Development

Buchanan, Paul C. "Laboratory Training and Organizational Development." ADMINISTRATIVE SCIENCE QUARTERLY 14, no. 3 (1969): 466-80.

Buchanan reviews studies from 1964-68 which used laboratory training in human relations programs to enhance the effectiveness of organizations.

The author believes that laboratory training facilitates personal growth and development, and thus can be of value to the individual who participates. Also, it accomplishes changes in individuals which, according to several theories, are important in changing and managing organizations.

The studies present a mixed picture of the effectiveness of laboratory training. "The evidence rather clearly indicates that laboratory training has a predictable and significant impact on most participants; yet it is also clear that from the standpoint of organizational improvement, laboratory training by itself is not enough," Buchanan writes.

Topics

Human Relations Training   Laboratory Training

Bunker, Douglas R. "Individual Application of Laboratory Training." JOURNAL OF APPLIED BEHAVIORAL SCIENCE 1, no. 2 (1965): 131-47.

Bunker presents data from a study of perceived behavior changes one year after participation in training. Coworkers saw participants as increasing significantly more than controls in cognitive openness, behavioral skill, and understanding of social processes. Long-range changes were correlated with learning measures at time of training.

Findings indicated that "the long-term outcomes of laboratory education tend to be increased capacity for adaptive orientation to their particular situation rather than the stereotyped enactment of an ideology. The roots of such behavior changes lie in improved methods of collecting and processing information about the organizational environment and increased personal freedom to act upon the basis of that information."

"There is strong evidence that groups, individuals, and entire training programs have differential learning outcomes; but as yet there is no systematic evidence concerning the links between particular components and observed applications," Bunker states.

Topics

Adaptation   Laboratory Training
Data Collection   Transfer of Training
Durability of Training

Bunker, Douglas R., and Knowles, Eric S. "Comparison of Behavioral Changes Resulting from Human Relations Training Laboratories of Different Lengths." JOURNAL OF APPLIED BEHAVIORAL SCIENCE 3, no. 4 (1967): 505-23.

Behavioral changes in back-home settings are reported for groups of persons who participated in two- and three-week human relations laboratories. Changes are reported by means of a behavior change description questionnaire (Bunker, above) given eight to ten months after training. The questionnaire was completed by the subject and seven coworkers (superiors, peers, and subordinates).

The authors derived two interrelated measures of change from the questionnaires: the "total change score," composed of the total number of different changes mentioned by a subject and his co-workers; and the "verified change score," composed of those behavior changes which are mentioned by two or more persons in a set of descriptions.

The authors note: "Both the perceived change score and the verified change score reveal more changes made by the three-week sample. . . . The three-week laboratory participants made more overt, proactive changes, as opposed to the more passive, attitudinal changes made by the two-week sample."

Topics

Attitude/Attitude Change   Human Relations Training
Behavior Change   Transfer of Training
Behavior Change Description
   Questionnaire

Burke, Richard L., and Bennis, Warren G. "Changes in Perception of Self and Others during Human Relations Training." HUMAN RELATIONS 14 (1961): 165-82.

Participants in three-week human relations training groups completed the Group Semantic Differential instrument during the middle of the first week and the latter part of the third week. Each participant completed the nineteen bipolar ratings for self, ideal, and other.

A factor analysis of the instrument showed three factors that accounted for 86 percent of the total variance: friendliness-evaluation, dominance-potency, and participation-activity.

Significant changes over time were found in the perception of group members, as follows: profile similarity between perceived actual self and perceived ideal self increased, changes in perceived actual self, were greater than changes in perceived ideal self; profile similarity between the individual's perceived actual self and mean perception of him by others increased; changes in the perception of the individual by others were greater than changes in the individual's perception of actual self; variance between members, in their perception of individuals on the participation-activity dimension, decreased.

Topics

Group Semantic Differential   Self-Concept
Instrument
Human Relations Training

Campbell, John P., and Dunnette, Marvin D. "Effectiveness of T-group Experiences in Managerial Training and Development." PSYCHOLOGICAL BULLETIN 70, no. 2 (1968): 73-104.

This article gives an in-depth review of research studies relating T-group experiences to the behavior of individuals in organizations. The stated objectives of the method and its technological elements are summarized, and speculation is offered about the nature and viability of implicit assumptions underlying T-group training.

Topics

Laboratory Training   Transfer of Training
T-Group

Carron, Theodore J. "Human Relations Training and Attitude Change: A Vector Analysis." PERSONNEL PSYCHOLOGY 17 (1964): 403-24.

Supervisors from research, development, and engineering units of a chemical company participated in human relations training over a six-month period. Attitude change in this group was compared with change in twelve matched controls who had no training.

The Leadership Opinion Questionnaire and F-scale were used to measure structure, consideration, and authoritarianism at four points in time: before training, at the end of training, six months after the end of training, and seventeen months after the training had ended.

Different analyses showed different results. Mean scores showed temporary changes toward democratic attitudes on authoritarianism scales greater in the experimental group than among the controls. The means after seventeen months showed no differences. A vector analysis showed significant change toward democratic attitudes in members of the experimental group but not in the controls.

Topics

Attitude/Attitude Change   F-Scale
Authoritarianism   Human Relations Training
Consideration   Leadership Opinion Questionnaire
Durability of Change   Structure

102

Clark, James V., and Culbert, Samuel A. "Mutually Therapeutic Perception and Self-Awareness in a T-group." JOURNAL OF APPLIED BEHAVIORAL SCIENCE 1, no. 2 (1965): 180-94.

The first author trained a group of students in two two-hour sessions each week for sixteen weeks. The group was studied to test two hypotheses: (1) Some members would show higher Problem Expression Scale (PES) ratings of samples of their speech near the end of their group experience than at the beginning, and (2) The members showing the most PES improvement will be those members who enter into the most interpersonal relationships in which the members perceive one another as high in level of regard, empathy, congruence, and unconditionality of regard.

Hypothesis 1 was supported. Two judges whose ratings were reliably correlated produced ratings which yielded positively significant changes for four Ss, nonsignificant change for five Ss, and a significant X^2s relating positive process scale changes to the number of dyadic relationships an S had in which both members perceived each other as high in therapeutic qualities.

The data suggest that the T-group "is a genuine therapeutic experience, although some have contended that T-groups and therapy groups are different. Furthermore, the present research not only supports the theory that interpersonal behavior is the prime determinant of therapeutic growth, it goes on to suggest that untrained laymen, given the proper context, can and do act therapeutically toward one another."

Topics

Laboratory Training	T-Group
Problem Expression Scale	Therapy
Self-Awareness	

Cooper, Cary L. "How Psychologically Dangerous are T-groups and Encounter Groups?" HUMAN RELATIONS 28, no. 3 (1975): 249-60.

Cooper gives a brief summary of studies on the dangers inherent in T-group or encounter group participation.

Topics

Encounter Group	T-Group

Culbert, Samuel A. "Accelerating Laboratory Learning Through a Phase Progression Model for Trainer Intervention." JOURNAL OF APPLIED BEHAVIORAL SCIENCE 6, no. 1 (1970): 21-38.

A description of a method for influencing the pace of T-groups is presented. A weekend group composed of trainers' wives is described with reference to the phase progression model.

The phase progression model contains four basic elements: explicit commitment to specific training goals; specified phases for group progression; technology for facilitating within-phase processes; and a method for shifting the group's focus from one phase to the next.

At the end of each phase the trainer intervened with comments referring to the previous phase, the current phase, and the future (next to evolve) phase.

Topics

Group Development   Laboratory Training
Group Processes   T-Group

Deep, Samuel D.; Bass, Bernard M.; and Vaughan, James A. "Some Effects on Business Gaming of Previous Quasi T-group Affiliations." JOURNAL OF APPLIED PSYCHOLOGY 51, no. 5 (1967): 426-31.

Success in a business game is used as a means of judging the effects of familiarity, cohesiveness, and ease of communications among members of a working group.

The findings were contrary to expectations. They suggest that in groups called upon to make many complex decisions under time pressure, the familiarity, cohesiveness, and ease of communications generated by common previous T-group experience may hinder rather than help generate adequate decisions.

Topics

Decision Making   T-Group

Dunnette, Marvin D. "People Feeling: Joy More Joy, and the 'Slough of Despond.'" JOURNAL OF APPLIED BEHAVIORAL SCIENCE 5, no. 1 (1969): 25-44.

Dunnette states that even though there is general disenchantment with studies done on T-groups, they probably are effective in changing behaviors in back-home settings.

A major goal of T-groups is described as follows: "to make perceivers more aware of their own perceptual filters, to help them be more aware of and sensitive to the attributes of Specific Others in their social worlds."

Dunnette discusses a study that tested whether an increased ability to differentiate among others was developed in T-groups. The study contained both T-groups and control groups that met for the same periods of time but engaged in different activities. Paper-and-pencil instruments and tapes were used to assess changes.

Greater empathy developed in groups showing more and a higher quality of interpersonal interaction. This increase was not a result of perceiver's adopting strategies of stereotype or assumed similarity, but was instead "a measure of their increased ability to differentiate accurately among Specific Others in their group."

Topics

Empathy   T-Group
Perception

_____. "Should Your People Take Sensitivity Training?" INNOVATION 14
(1970): 42-55.

Six stages of T-group development are presented: escaping from
loneliness; providing warmth and support; learning sensory and emotional sensitivity and being able to tolerate anxiety; understanding
oneself and others; learning to change interpersonal behavior; and
resolving conflicts.

Stages one through three are described as recreational stages. Four
through six are learning stages.

Problems can develop if: (1) The leader fails to state his objectives.
(2) The group fails to pass through early stages in an attempt to
reach stage four. (3) Groups do not get past the diagnostic stages
to behavioral reeducation. (4) Trainers are hung up at certain
stages and cannot take the group beyond them.

Dunnette argues against including people from the same organization in the same group.

Topics

Diagnosis/Evaluation   Sensitivity Training
Group Development   T-Group
Learning   Trainer

Dunnette, Marvin D., and Campbell, John P. "Laboratory Education: Impact
on People and Organizations." In ORGANIZATIONAL CHANGE AND DEVEL-
OPMENT, edited by Gene W. Dalton, Paul R. Lawrence, and Larry E. Greiner,
pp. 347-76. Homewood, Ill.: Irwin-Dorsey, 1970.

This chapter is based on a thorough review of the laboratory training literature.

"By laboratory education we mean those personnel and organizational development and training courses which combine traditional
training features--such as lectures, group problem-solving sessions,
and role-playing--with T-group or sensitivity training techniques,"
the authors write.

"There is little firm evidence of any significant changes in attitude,
outlook, orientation, or view of others as a result of T-group
training. . . . Evidence in favor of any claims that laboratory
education can increase or change interpersonal awareness, 'self-
insight,' or interpersonal sensitivity is very nearly nonexistent.

"The evidence of training-produced changes in job behavior,
though present, is severely limited by two major considerations we
have mentioned. First, the many sources of bias constitute com-

peting explanations for the results obtained. Second, none of the studies yields any evidence that the change in job behavior have any favorable effect on actual performance effectiveness.

"In spite of . . . essentially negative results on objective measures, individuals who have been trained by laboratory education methods are more likely to be seen as changing their job behavior than are individuals in similar job settings who have not been trained. These reported changes are in the direction of more openness, better self- and interpersonal understanding, and improved communications and leadership skills."

(See also Campbell and Dunnette, above.)

Topics

Attitude/Attitude Change	Self-Awareness
Behavior Change	Sensitivity Training
Communications	T-Group
Laboratory Training	Transfer of Training
Leadership	

Golembiewski, Robert T. "Planned Organizational Change: A Major Emphasis in a Behavioral Approach to Administration." In SENSITIVITY TRAINING AND THE LABORATORY APPROACH, edited by Robert T. Golembiewski and Arthur Blumberg, pp. 361-90. Itasca, Ill.: F.E. Peacock, 1970.

The laboratory approach to organizational change is emphasized. Topics discussed include types of interventions, necessary skills and values, limitations, and a description of three applications.

According to this author, the laboratory approach may be used for three major purposes: modifying the problem-solving perspectives of individuals on work-related issues; modifying organizational styles by inducing changes in interpersonal and group behavior; and modifying the attitudes of individuals in organizations toward more effective performance.

Topics

Attitude/Attitude Change	Problem Solving
Intervention	Skill
Laboratory Approach	Values

_____. RENEWING ORGANIZATIONS: THE LABORATORY APPROACH TO PLANNED CHANGE. Itasca, Ill.: F.E. Peacock, 1972. ix, 593 p.

This book deals with change, and how individuals and organizations can make more effective choices, as well as cope better with the changes thrust upon them. Emphasis is on a technology for renewal and change.

Contents

Introduction
Part I: Some Orienting Perspectives

Section A: The Laboratory Approach to Learning: Schema of a Method

Section B: The Laboratory Approach to Learning: Values That Guide Applications

Section C: The Laboratory Approach to Organization Development: Perspectives on Theory and Practice

Section D: The Laboratory Approach to Organization Development (II): Further Perspectives on Theory and Practice

Part II: Some Applications for Individuals in Organizations

Section A: Interventions Aimed at Individuals: Common Processes and Their Consequences in Various Designs

Section B: Interventions Aimed at Individuals: Toward Applying Laboratory Values to Job and Career

Section C: Interventions Aimed at Groups: Some Developmental Trends

Section D: Interventions Aimed at Groups: Three Basic Approaches to Change

Section E: Interventions Aimed at Complex Organizations: Changing Patterns of Interpersonal and Intergroup Relations

Section F: Interventions Aimed at Complex Organizations: Facilitating Crucial Linkages and Coordination

Part III: Some Sense of Future Challenges

Section A: Patterns for the Future: Toward the Adaptive Organization

Section B: Kaleidoscopes of the Future: Changing Orders at Work, at Play, in Life

Topics

Bureaucracy	Problem Analysis Questionnaire
Change Agent	Process Consultation
Change Technology	Risk/Risk Taking
Climate	Sensitivity Training
Conflict/Conflict Resolution	Sociotechnical Systems
Confrontation	Stranger Laboratory
Encounter Group	Structural Changes
Feedback	Survey Feedback
FIRO-B	Team Building/Development
Group Development	T-Group
Job Design	Third-Party Intervention
Job Enrichment	TORI
Johari Window	Trust
Laboratory Approach	Unfreezing
Matrix Organization	Values
Merger Laboratory	Work Group
Organization Development	

Golembiewski, Robert T., and Blumberg, Arthur. SENSITIVITY TRAINING AND THE LABORATORY APPROACH. Itasca, Ill.: F.E. Peacock, 1970. 514 p.

Each chapter of this large collection of readings begins with an introduction by the authors. The thirty-seven articles cover a wide range of issues discussed by major contributors to this area.

Contents

Contributing Authors

Argyris, C.	Hampton-Turner, C.M.	Mouton, J.S.
Barnes, L.B.	Harrison, R.	Odiorne, G.S.
Bass, B.M.	Horwitz, L.	Rogers, C.R.
Bennis, W.G.	Horwitz, M.	Seashore, C.
Bessell, H.	House, R.J.	Shepard, H.A.
Blake, R.	Jenkins, D.H.	Skousen, W.C.
Bradford, L.P.	Klaw, S.	Stock, D.
Clark, J.V.	Lippitt, G.L.	Tannenbaum, R.
Culbert, S.A.	Luke, B.	This, L.E.
Deep, S.D.	Massarik, F.	Vaughan, J.A.
Friedlander, F.	Mial, H.C.	Walton, R.E.
Greiner, L.E.	Miles, M.B.	Weschler, I.R.

Topics

Change Agent	Laboratory Approach
Collaboration	Leadership
Conflict	Managerial Grid
Confrontation	Self-Concept
Defensiveness	Sensitivity Training
Diagnosis/Evaluation	Trainer
Feedback	Transfer of Training
Group Development	

Golembiewski, Robert T., and Carrigan, Stokes B. "Planned Change in Organization Style Based on the Laboratory Approach." ADMINISTRATIVE SCIENCE QUARTERLY 15, no. 1 (1970): 79-93.

This is a report on the design and results of an effort to change the organization style of a sales unit in a business organization. Likert's profile of organizational characteristics was used to measure changes in organization style. A one-week learning experience produced significant changes in self-reports by managers about the style of interpersonal and intergroup relations in the organiza-

tion. The "entire managerial population was exposed to the learning design, so that there was no control group. Therefore, the
changes in self-reports can only be tentatively attributed to the
experimental design, rather than to random factors or the passage
of time."

Topics

Influence   Laboratory Approach
Intergroup   Organization Style
Interpersonal Processes

Hampton-Turner, C.M.   "An Existential 'Learning Theory' and the Integration
of T-group Research."   JOURNAL OF APPLIED BEHAVIORAL SCIENCE 2, no.
4 (1966): 367-86.

A theory is presented to integrate findings from studies evaluating
learning in T-groups. Three such studies are integrated with the
theory.

Topics

Learning   T-Group

Hartley, Dianna; Roback, Howard B.; and Abramowitz, Stephen I.   "Deteriora-
tion Effects in Encounter Groups."   AMERICAN PSYCHOLOGIST 31, no. 3
(1976): 247-55.

This examination of potential negative outcomes resulting from encounter group experiences covers the types and incidence of casualties reported; participant, group, and leader variables associated
with negative outcome; procedures for minimizing casualties; and
research considerations.

Topics

Encounter Group   Leadership
Feedback   Sensitivity Training
Laboratory Training   T-Group

House, Robert J.   "T-group Education and Leadership Effectiveness: A Review
of the Empiric Literature and a Critical Evaluation." PERSONNEL PSYCHOL-
OGY 20, no. 1 (1967): 1-32.

House reviews the T-group literature. He gives special emphasis
to the effective use of groups and ethical concerns inherent in the
T-group approach.

Topics

Ethics   T-Group
Leadership

Kolb, David A.; Winter, Sara K.; and Berlew, David E.   "Self-directed

Change: Two Studies." JOURNAL OF APPLIED BEHAVIORAL SCIENCE 4, no. 4 (1968): 453-71.

Graduate students participated in four T-groups run on a self-directed change model. The groups took part in three different experimental conditions which varied in the period (but not total time) of the group activities, the presence or absence of feedback, and sensitization to the issues of commitment.

Based on self-reports and trainers' ratings it was determined that the highly committed subjects "felt as though they changed more [and] also showed more observable changes in behavior than did low-commitment subjects. . . . T-Group feedback relevant to an individual's change project facilitates self-perceived change. . . . While degree of change is not related to the amount of feedback in the first half of the T-Group, it appears to be positively related to the amount of feedback given in the second half of the T-Group."

Topics

Commitment	Self-Change
Feedback	T-Group

Kuriloff, Arthur H., and Atkins, Stuart. "T-group for a Work Team." JOURNAL OF APPLIED BEHAVIORAL SCIENCE 2, no. 1 (1966): 63-94.

A case history is presented documenting the use of T-group training in a small manufacturing company. A day-by-day account is provided with excerpts from each of the five days.

Findings suggest that effective results in a T-group for a work team may be attained by "(1) a prior level of trust in the boss, (2) presence of the boss in all T-group sessions, (3) intensive and consecutive sessions followed by immediate application of learning on-the-job, (4) emphasis on improving individuals' inter-personal competence primarily for the sake of the business, (5) confronting of each person as seen by others, and self-disclosure of personal feelings between people."

Topics

Confrontation	T-Group
Interpersonal Competence	Transfer of Training
Self-Disclosure	Trust
Team Building/Development	

Lakin, Martin, and Carson, Robert C. "Participant Perception of Group Process in Group Sensitivity Training." INTERNATIONAL JOURNAL OF GROUP PSYCHOTHERAPY 14 (1964): 116-22.

This study set out to determine if the participant perceived a standard recurring developmental sequence in sensitivity training groups over the total training experience. The findings conclude that group experience may be no less unique than individual experience.

Topics

Group Development   Sensitivity Training
Group Processes

Lubin, Bernard, and Zuckerman, Marvin. "Level of Emotional Arousal in Laboratory Training." JOURNAL OF APPLIED BEHAVIORAL SCIENCE 5, no. 4 (1969): 483-90.

The relative level of stress created in T-groups was evaluated through a study including the participants of four one-week groups and participants of a study on perceptual isolation.

The researchers developed an adjective checklist to determine anxiety, depression, and hostility. Since members of the T-groups were found to be different from those of the perceptual isolation study, the investigators used analysis of covariance procedures.

The level of stress was found to be less in the members of the T-groups (none of the participants reached a level considered to represent unusually high stress) than in those participating in the perceptual isolation study (35 percent reached the level of high stress).

Topics

Laboratory Training   T-Group
Stress

Miles, Matthew B. "Changes During and Following Laboratory Training: A Clinical Experimental Study." JOURNAL OF APPLIED BEHAVIORAL SCIENCE 1, no. 3 (1965): 215-42.

The experimental subjects in this study were thirty-four elementary school principals who participated in two-week NTL laboratories. Controls (148) consisted of a group of randomly chosen elementary school principals and another group·selected through peer nominations.

A series of instruments were administered to all participants before the laboratories, three months after the laboratories, and eight months after the laboratories. Measures were also taken during the laboratories to determine sensitivity, diagnostic ability, and action skills.

"Substantively, we have found valid experimental-control differences as a result of a human relations training experience; the gains by participants were primarily predicted by variables connected with actual participation in the treatment--unfreezing, active involvement, and reception of feedback. The personality variables studied --ego strength, flexibility, and need affiliation--did not affect laboratory outcomes directly, but did seem to influence behavior during training. Finally, the organizational variables studied-- personal security, autonomy and power, and organizational problem-

solving adequacy--had less impact on the participants' stance at
the beginning of training than expected, but did appear to affect
their subsequent use of learnings on the job."

Topics

Autonomy	Laboratory Training
Diagnosis/Evaluation	Participation
Feedback	Power
Flexibility	Problem Solving
Human Relations Training	Security

NTL Institute for Applied Behavioral Science. "What to Observe in a T-Group."
In SENSITIVITY TRAINING AND THE LABORATORY APPROACH, edited by
Robert T. Golembiewski and Arthur Blumberg, pp. 86-90. Itasca, Ill.: F.E.
Peacock, 1970.

Various types and levels of interactions deemed significant in T-
groups are summarized. Included are issues of content and process;
communications; decision-making procedures; task, maintenance,
and self-oriented behavior; and emotional issues.

Topics

Communications	Process
Content	Self-Oriented Behavior
Decision Making	Task
Group Processes	T-Group
Maintenance	

Odiorne, George S. "The Trouble with Sensitivity Training." In SENSITIVITY
TRAINING AND THE LABORATORY APPROACH, edited by Robert T. Golembiewski and Arthur Blumberg, pp. 273-87. Itasca, Ill.: F.E. Peacock, 1970.

Odiorne presents a negative evaluation of sensitivity training as
a useful training technique. He attacks what he views as a failure
to define desired terminal behaviors. He adds that since these
behaviors are not clear, it is impossible to establish the logical
steps essential to good training or to evaluate the success of such
training.

Topics

Behavior Change	Sensitivity Training
Organization Goal/Task	Value Change

Oshry, Barry, and Harrison, Roger. "Transfer from Here-and-Now to There-
and-Then: Changes in Organizational Problem Diagnosis Stemming from T-group
Training." JOURNAL OF APPLIED BEHAVIORAL SCIENCE 2, no. 2 (1966):
185-98.

The study focuses on changes in the participants' abilities to diagnose interpersonal work problems in organizational settings.

Forty-six middle-level managers participated in two-week T-groups. Each participant completed the Problem Analysis Questionnaire on the first and the next-to-last day of training.

The results indicate that as the manager prepares to return home from the training "(1) His work world seems to him to be more human and less impersonal. (2) He sees clearer connections between how well interpersonal needs are met and how well work gets done. (3) He sees himself clearly as the most significant part of his work problems. (4) He sees no clear connection between his new perceptions and how he translates these into action."

The authors note that they have not determined the effect that "seeing things differently" has on organizational behavior.

Topics

Diagnosis/Evaluation	Problem Analysis Questionnaire
Interpersonal Processes	T-Group
Perception	Transfer of Training

Psathas, George, and Hardert, Ronald. "Trainer Intervention and Normative Patterns in the T-group." JOURNAL OF APPLIED BEHAVIORAL SCIENCE 2, no. 2 (1966): 149-69.

In a study of seven two-week T-groups, the authors isolated several categories of normative dimensions into which trainer interventions can be reliably classified. These categories include analysis of group interaction or process; feelings; feedback; acceptance concern; participation; goal and task concern; trainer membership-- authority problems; leadership behavior; structure concern; behavior experimentation; and decision making. The first four categories received the greatest emphasis in the groups studied.

Topics

Decision Making	Norms
Feedback	Participation
Group Processes	T-Group
Intervention	Trainer
Leadership	

Rogers, Carl R. CARL ROGERS ON ENCOUNTER GROUPS. New York: Harper & Row, 1970. 172 p.

Rogers touches upon several aspects of encounter groups, including theoretical bases, reasons for their increased acceptance, typical stages and processes, and the use of this technique for the purpose of changing individual behavior and the functioning of institutions.

Contents

1. The origin and scope of the trend toward "Groups"
2. The process of the encounter group
3. Can I be a facilitative person in a group?

4. Change after encounter groups: In persons, in relationships, in
   organizations
5. The person in change: The process as experienced
6. The lonely person--and his experiences in an encounter group
7. What we know from research
8. Areas of application
9. Building facilitative skills
10. What of the future?

Topics

Encounter Group   Group Processes
Group Development   Trainer

Schein, Edgar H., and Bennis, Warren G. PERSONAL AND ORGANIZATION-
AL CHANGE THROUGH GROUP METHODS. New York: John Wiley & Sons,
1965. 376 p.

Schein and Bennis have included both their own conceptualizations
and those of others concerned with laboratory training. Descriptions are provided of the assumptions, objectives, processes, and
outcomes of this educational strategy.

Contents

Part One: What Is Laboratory Training?
    1. Introduction
    2. What is laboratory training: Description of a typical
       residential laboratory
    3. Overview of laboratory training
Part Two: The Uses of Laboratory Training
    4. Variations in laboratory training
    5. The design of one-week laboratories
    6. Sensitivity training and being motivated
    7. The use of the laboratory method in a psychiatric
       hospital
    8. A 9,9 approach for increasing organizational produc-
       tivity
    9. Sensitivity training and community development
    10. Principles and strategies in the use of laboratory
        training for improving social systems
Part Three: Research on Laboratory Training Outcomes
    11. Research on laboratory training outcomes
    12. Learning processes and outcomes in human relations
        training: A clinical experimental study
    13. The effect of laboratory education upon individual
        behavior
Part Four: A Theory of Learning Through Laboratory Training
    14. A general overview of our learning theory
    15. Organizational forces that aid and hinder attitude
        change
    16. The laboratory as a force toward learning

17. Some hypotheses about the relative learning impact of different kinds of laboratories
18. Our questions about laboratory training

Contributing Authors

Blake, R.	Johnson, D.L.	Mouton, J.S.
Bugental, J.F.T.	Klein, D.C.	Moyer, R.
Bunker, D.R.	Lyle, F.A.	Oshry, B.
Hanson, P.G.	Miles, M.B.	Rothaus, P.
Harrison, R.	Morton, R.B.	Tannenbaum, R.

Topics

Adaptation	Human Relations Training
Affect	Interpersonal Competence
Attitude/Attitude Change	Laboratory Training
Change Agent	Learning
Changing	Refreezing
Cognition	Role
Collaboration	Self-Awareness
Communications	Sensitivity Training
Diagnosis/Evaluation	Skill
Feedback	T-Group
Group Processes	Unfreezing
Here-and-Now Data	

Schutz, William C., and Allen, Vernon L. "The Effects of a T-group Laboratory on Interpersonal Behavior." JOURNAL OF APPLIED BEHAVIORAL SCIENCE 2, no. 3 (1966): 265-86.

Focusing on changes in interpersonal relations, this study involved seventy-one persons participating in two-week human relations training laboratories and thirty university students as controls.

The FIRO-B instrument was administered before the laboratory began, immediately after the laboratory had terminated, and six months later. In addition, an open-ended questionnaire was used during the last data collection period.

Results from these instruments supported the hypothesis that "the training laboratory changes people selectively, depending on their initial personality, the overly dominant becoming less dominant, the overly affectionate more discriminating, and so on. The hypothesis was also supported that change after a period of six months is in a positive direction with respect to the participant's self-concepts and behavior and feelings toward other people, as well as the behavior toward the participant."

Topics

Durability of Change	Laboratory Training
FIRO-B	Self-Concept
Human Relations Training	T-Group
Interpersonal Processes	

Stock, Dorothy. "A Survey of Research on T-Groups." In T-GROUP THEORY AND LABORATORY METHOD, edited by Jack R. Gibb, and Kenneth D. Benne, pp. 395-441. New York: John Wiley & Sons, 1964.

A review of pre-1964 T-group studies provides the basis for an exploration of several issues, including the course of development in the T-group; the effects of group composition; the character of T-groups as described by members; the role of the trainer; individual behavior in the T-group; members' perceptions of one another; and the impact of the T-group on individual learning and change.

Topics

Group Composition	Laboratory Training
Group Development	Learning
Group Processes	T-Group
Individual Change	Trainer

Valiquet, Michael I. "Individual Change in a Management Development Program." JOURNAL OF APPLIED BEHAVIORAL SCIENCE 4, no. 3 (1968): 313-25.

The study described focuses on the adaptation of behavioral changes to organizational settings. The methodology follows that of Bunker (See p. 100), with the exception that family groups were used in this study and stranger groups were used by Bunker.

Results indicate that "participants are seen by co-workers as increasing significantly more than controls in effective initiation and assertiveness, in capacity for collaboration and operational skill in interpersonal relations, and in diagnostic awareness of self and the ability to fulfill perceived needs."

It is noteworthy that "the greater number of significant changes observed in this study occurred in the overt, operational categories rather than in the inferred, attitudinal categories, as was more the case in Bunker's study." The author attributes this difference to the different natures of the groups, the program goals, and the environment of change.

Topics

Attitude/Attitude Change	Interpersonal Processes
Change Goals	Laboratory Training
Collaboration	Management Training/Development
Diagnosis/Evaluation	Self-Awareness
Environment	Stranger Laboratory
Family Laboratory	Transfer of Training

Wagner, Alan B. "The Use of Process Analysis in Business Decision Games." JOURNAL OF APPLIED BEHAVIORAL SCIENCE 1, no. 4 (1965): 387-408.

The article describes a study in which a four-day sensitivity training laboratory was included as the second part of an executive development conference. At the end of the training the participants played a business game.

The game consisted of several segments, each concluding in participant analysis of the process by which decisions were made.

The author identifies three stages of group development executed by participants in decision-making processes: regression, overcompensation, and realistic problem solving.

It is suggested that the use of gaming techniques may be a way to build bridges to the back-home environment.

Topics

Gaming
Group Processes
Laboratory Training
Overcompensation
Problem Solving

Process Analysis
Regression
Sensitivity Training
Transfer of Training

Winn, Alexander. "The Laboratory Approach to Organization Development: A Tentative Model of Planned Change." THE JOURNAL OF MANAGEMENT STUDIES, May 1969, pp. 155-66.

Description of various forms (e.g., family laboratories, stranger laboratories, work team laboratories) of laboratory training employed by Alcani Canada are presented, together with the judged usefulness of each form in organization development. The theme is that the more the laboratory takes the actual work group as its focus, the higher is the potential for the transfer of learnings. This is based on the proposition that "programmes of team development contribute substantially to individual growth but . . . the reverse is not necessarily true. The explicit purpose of the work team or organizational family laboratory is the discovery of new interdependencies . . . and location of existing interdependencies which are not working too effectively."

Topics

Change Agent
Change Strategy
Consultant
Cousins Laboratory

Laboratory Training
Stranger Laboratory
T-Group
Transfer of Training

MANAGEMENT BY OBJECTIVES

Ivancevich, John M. "A Longitudinal Assessment of Management by Objectives." ADMINISTRATIVE SCIENCE QUARTERLY 17, no. 1 (1972): 126-38.

A review of the available empirically based literature focusing on management by objectives (MBO) programs led the author to conclude that long term effects of MBO are unknown. Longitudinal data are presented from a study examining the effects of MBO programs in two medium-sized firms.

"The findings suggest that an active participation role by management in the design and implementation of MBO can have a significant impact on improving the overall job satisfaction of managers. The crucial point is that some form of reinforcement of what was learned and practiced in the training sessions is necessary."

Results also suggest that time is a critical variable in assessing the impact of such programs. In this study short-run results suggest different conclusions than do long-run results. The author concludes that the ability of MBO programs to improve organizations in the long-run is in doubt. "Until more tightly controlled research is conducted, organizations will have to assume that MBO is or is not an effective procedure for improving job satisfaction and/or performance," he writes.

Topics

Management by Objectives	Porter Job Satisfaction
Motivation	Questionnaire
Performance	Satisfaction

Odiorne, George S. MANAGEMENT BY OBJECTIVES. New York: Pitman, 1965. 204 p.

After pointing out the future needs for management, Odiorne describes the system of management by objectives: "Management by objectives provides for the maintenance and orderly growth of the organization by means of statements of what is expected for everyone involved, and measurement of what is actually achieved."

The system is envisioned as an aid toward overcoming the following problems: measuring the true contribution of managerial and professional personnel, defining common goals, and defining areas of responsibility. In addition, management by objectives is designed to eliminate the need for people to change their personalities and provide a means of determining each manager's span of control.

Contents

1. The new look in management
2. A flight from capitalism?
3. The decline of risk bearing
4. The system of management by objectives
5. Installing the system
6. Measuring organization performance
7. Setting routine and emergency goals
8. Setting creative goals
9. Setting personal development goals
10. How much subordinate participation in goal-setting?
11. Relating salary administration to management by objectives
12. The problem of the annual performance review
13. Assessing potential

Topics

Goals (Individual/
    Organizational)
Leadership
Management

Management by Objectives
Measurement
Responsibility

MANAGERIAL GRID ORGANIZATION DEVELOPMENT

Blake, Robert R., and Mouton, Jane S. BUILDING A DYNAMIC CORPO-
RATION THROUGH GRID ORGANIZATIONAL DEVELOPMENT. Reading,
Mass.: Addison-Wesley, 1969. 120 p.

This is a presentation of organizational development based largely
on Blake and Mouton's development of the managerial grid. They
stress development as the process of closing the gap between what
is and what should be. The gap is closed through systematic development. Six phases of development are suggested as necessary
for fulfilling essential conditions for systematic development.

The approach outlined stresses involvement by the participants in
all phases. "The whole learning situation is based on a self-
convincing approach. It is a process of self-discovery, self-testing,
self-comparison, self-judgment, and self-evaluation."

The integration of the individual and the organization is a major
theme. "Organization development has a major objective of
strengthening the capacities of corporations to utilize people to
permit the sound merging of self-interests with corporate interests.
Corporate excellence is approached when this merger has been
achieved. . . . Corporate excellence and the excellence of individuals are one and the same."

Topics

Conflict/Conflict Resolution
Goals (Individual/Organizational)

Grid Organizational
Development

_____. THE MANAGERIAL GRID. Houston: Gulf Publishing Co., 1964.
340 p.

The Managerial Grid is described and presented as "an inclusive
statement for orienting managerial actions" (p. x). This volume
"compares alternatives available to a manager in achieving production through people, . . . provides a way for aiding the reader
to measure his own managerial style, . . . defines the behavioral
requirements of shifting any one style toward any other . . . [and]
pictures how, through educational effort, an entire system . . .
can change its culture and raise itself by its bootstraps toward organization excellence" (p. xi).

Contents

1. Self Assessment of Key Managerial Orientations

2. The Managerial Dilemma
3. The 9,1 Managerial Style
4. The 1,9 Managerial Style
5. The 1,1 Managerial Style
6. The 5,5 Managerial Style
7. The 9,9 Managerial Style
8. Managerial Facades
9. Mixed Grid Theories
10. Career Accomplishment and Managerial Style
11. Analyzing Personal Managerial Style
12. A 9,9 Approach to Organization Development
13. Organization Development and Performance
14. Trends and Practices of Management

Topics

Attitude/Attitude Change
Change Strategy
Communications
Conflict/Conflict Resolution
Decision Making
Diagnosis Evaluation
Goals (Individual/Organizational)
Laboratory Training

Leadership
Management
Management Training/
    Development
Managerial Grid
Motivation
Resistance to Change
Satisfaction
Trust

Blake, Robert [R.], et al. "Breakthrough in Organizational Development." HARVARD BUSINESS REVIEW 42, no. 6 (1964): 133-55.

The grid program was used in an attempt to change attitudes, values, and behaviors in a company employing 4,000 persons. An evaluation of the program was conducted by researchers not involved in the change effort.

Organizational records and anonymous survey questionnaires assessed outcomes. Data collection procedures started after the first phase of the effort was completed. The results showed increased productivity per employee; decreased controllable costs; doubled profits; perceived improvement in group performance; promotion criteria changes; perceived improvement in intergroup and interdepartmental relationships; and attitudes shifting to be more congruent with the grid 9,9 model.

Topics

Grid Organizational
    Development

Managerial Grid

MOTIVATION TRAINING

Aronoff, Joel, and Litwin, George H. "Achievement Motivation Training and

Executive Advancement." JOURNAL OF APPLIED BEHAVIORAL SCIENCE 7, no. 2 (1971): 215-29.

An experimental study describes the effects of achievement motivation training on promotions and raises of middle-level managers. Two partially matched groups were used. The sixteen members of the experimental groups participated in a one-week motivation training course. Members of the control group participated in a four-week management development course.

Unusual rates of advancement (job level and salary) were examined two years after the courses were given. Five members of the experimental group were not available at this time. "The results . . show that the relative performances of those executives who attended the Achievement training course evidence a significantly higher rate of advancement than the control group."

According to J.R. Hurley, "Science and Fiction in Executive Training" (see pp. 230-33 of the same journal), the results are not clear. Several methodological problems are demonstrated which favor the authors' position.

Topics

Management Training/
Development

Motivation Training
Need Achievement

ORGANIZATIONAL DESIGN

Galbraith, Jay. DESIGNING COMPLEX ORGANIZATIONS. Reading, Mass.: Addison-Wesley, 1973. xii, 150 p.

One of three 1973 additions to the original (1969) Addison-Wesley OD series, this volume attempts to present "an analytical framework of the design of organizations and particularly of types of organizations which apply lateral decision processes or matrix forms" (p. vii). A primary assumption of this book is that although lateral information processes do not always arise spontaneously, they can be designed. Based on the various works of J.D. Thompson and H. Simon, Galbraith provides a theoretical basis and case illustrations "to identify types of matrix designs and the conditions under which they are appropriate" (p. vii).

Contents

1. Introduction
2. Information Processing Model
3. Information Reduction Strategies
4. Alternative 3: Investment in a Vertical Information System
5. Alternative 4: Creation of Lateral Relations
6. A Case Study--Teams

7. Lateral Relations: Integrating Roles and Matrix Designs
8. Review of Model and Empirical Evidence
9. Case Studies
10. Authority and Responsibility in Lateral Relations

Topics

Authority	Matrix Organization
Bureaucracy	Mechanistic Systems
Change Strategy	Organic Systems
Communications	Organization Design
Decision Making	Role
	Uncertainty

Kilmann, Ralph H. "An Organic-Adaptive Organization: The MAPS Method." PERSONNEL 51 (May-June 1974): 35-47.

The rationale and procedures are presented for a method of organization design based on participative management, management by objectives, management of interdependencies, and organization development. The basis for the designs emerging from this method are judgments of organizational members concerning both task competencies and interpersonal concerns. Organization development is seen as the method "necessary to translate the potential represented in the MAPS design into organizational behavior" (p. 44).

Topics

Adaptation	MAPS
Change Strategy	MAPS Questionnaire
Change Technology	Organic-Adaptive
Management by Objectives	Participation
	Participative Management

McKelvey, Bill, and Kilmann, Ralph H. "Organization Design: A Participative Multivariate Approach." ADMINISTRATIVE SCIENCE QUARTERLY 20, no. 1 (1975): 24-36.

A school of management was the setting for a study that had as its objective "the design of purposeful subunits through the use of multivariate, participative approaches based on a synthesis of the rational and natural system models of organization and on objectives of subunit formation" (p. 33). Inputs from all organizational members were used to maximize "homogeneity with regard to values and attitudes supporting group decision-making norms and minimize task-related interdependencies among subunits" (p. 28).

Topics

Organizational Design	Participation

PHYSICAL SETTING MODIFICATION

Steele, Fred I. PHYSICAL SETTINGS AND ORGANIZATIONAL DEVELOP-
MENT. Reading, Mass.: Addison-Wesley, 1973. 150 p.

The goals of this volume focusing on physical settings are to increase the environmental competence of both readers and those who
are influenced by readers, increase readers' awareness of an environmental crisis in our culture, indicate ways in which physical
environmental changes can be used as a means for starting or supporting social system changes, and stimulate further exploration in
the field of environment and behavior.

The core of this volume is organized around six functions of physical settings originating from Maslow's theory of human needs and
the author's observations. The six functions include: security and
shelter; social contact; symbolic identification; task instrumentality;
pleasure; and growth. A rating scheme with examples is provided
for evaluating settings according to the six functions.

Contents

Part One: An Orientation
   1. Basic Definitions
   2. Historical Connections between Organization Theory
      and Physical Design
Part Two: The Functions of Physical Settings
   3. An Introduction to the Function of Settings
   4. Function I: Shelter and Security
   5. Function II: Social Contact
   6. Function III: Symbolic Identification
   7. Function IV: Task Instrumentality
   8. Function V: Pleasure
   9. Function VI: Growth
   10. The Functions in Practice
Part Three: Toward Environmental Competence
   11. Environmental Competence: Concepts
   12. Enhancing Environmental Competence: Some Sug-
       gested Methods
   13. Organizational Environmental Competence: Spatial
       Decision Processes
   References

Topics

Change Strategy
Diagnosis/Evaluation
Environment
Growth

Norms
Process Consultation
Sociophysical Development
Sociotechnical System

PROCESS CONSULTATION

Schein, Edgar H. PROCESS CONSULTATION. Reading, Mass.: Addison-

Wesley, 1969. 147 p.

The role of process consultation in organizational development efforts is described. The primary focus of this volume is on group processes and interactions between the process consultant and the client group.

Contents

Part One: Diagnosis
1. Introduction
2. Human processes in organizations: An overview
3. Communication processes
4. Functional roles of group members
5. Group problem-solving and decision-making
6. Group norms and group growth
7. Leadership and authority
8. Intergroup processes

Part Two: Intervention
9. Establishing contact and defining a relationship
10. Selecting a setting and a method of work
11. Gathering data
12. Intervention
13. Evaluation of results and disengagement
14. Process consultation in perspective

Topics

Attitude/Attitude Change	Group Processes
Authority	Group Roles
Change Agent	Intergroup Processes
Communication	Intervention
Competition	Leadership
Cooperation	Norms
Counseling	Problem Solving
Decision Making	Process Consultation
Diagnosis/Evaluation	Skill
Feedback	Values

REWARD SYSTEM MODIFICATION

Lawler, Edward E. III, and Hackman, J. Richard. "Impact of Employee Participation in the Development of Pay Incentive Plans: A Field Experiment." JOURNAL OF APPLIED PSYCHOLOGY 53, no. 6 (1969): 467-71.

This is a study of the effects of employee involvement in the development of pay incentive plans. The subjects were part-time maintenance workers. Three autonomous work groups developed their own pay incentive plans to reward good attendance on the job (Condition A). These plans were then imposed by the company on other work groups (Condition B). There were two groups of control employees: one group discussed job attendance problems with the experimenters but received no additional experimental treatment, and the other received no treatment. A significant increase in attendance followed only Condition A. Possible reasons cited: (a) participation caused greater commitment to the plan; (b) employees who participated in the development of their plan were more knowledgeable about it; and (c) participation increased the employees' faith in the good intentions of management with respect to the plan.

Topics

Attendance   Pay Incentive
Commitment   Trust
Participation

Patten, Thomas H., Jr., and Fraser, Karen. "Using the Organizational Rewards System as an OD Lever: Case Study of a Data-based Intervention." JOURNAL OF APPLIED BEHAVIORAL SCIENCE 11, no. 4 (1975): 457-74.

A large manufacturing organization provides the setting for an OD intervention focusing on organizational reward systems. The primary intervention included data collection by means of a questionnaire followed by the feedback of results to top managers. "The findings of the study suggest that rewards system interventions can be fruitful, that the greatest rewards are often perceived by managerial and professional employees as inherent in the work itself, and that improvements in the tools (such as the Likert Profile) for studying the functions and dysfunctions of rewards systems are needed" (p. 457).

Topics

Change Strategy   Likert Profile
Feedback   Reward Systems

Scheflen, Kenneth C., Lawler, Edward E. III, and Hackman, J. Richard. "Long-term Impact of Employee Participation in the Development of Pay Incentive Plans: A Field Experiment Revisited." JOURNAL OF APPLIED PSYCHOLOGY 55, no. 3 (1971): 182-86.

"In an earlier study Lawler and Hackman examined the effects of worker participation in the development of pay incentive plans. In the original study, three work groups developed their own incentive plans to reward high attendance, and identical plans were then imposed by company management in two other work groups. A significant increase in attendance 'was found during the first 16 weeks following implementation of the plans only in the groups where the plans were participatively developed. Data reported in the present study cover a 12-week period beginning 1 year after the original plans had been installed. After the data reported in the earlier study had been collected, the incentive plans were discontinued by company management in two of the three participative groups. The present results show that attendance dropped below pretreatment levels in these two groups, and that attendance continued high in the third participative group. An increase in attendance was found after 1 year in those groups where incentive plans had been imposed by company management."

Topics

Attendance   Participation
Commitment   Pay Incentive
Durability of Change

SCANLON PLAN

Doyle, Robert J. "A New Look at the Scanlon Plan." MANAGEMENT ACCOUNTING 52 (September 1970): 48-52.

Doyle argues that the Scanlon Plan should be seriously considered as a means of tapping the unused human potential available in organizations.

According to this author, the Scanlon Plan provides a means for "increasing productivity by reducing manual labor." General steps for installation of this system are provided.

Topics

Change Technology   Scanlon Plan

SOCIOTECHNICAL SYSTEM DESIGN

Davis, Louis E., and Taylor, James C. DESIGN OF JOBS. Middlesex, Engl.: Penguin Books, 1972. 479 p.

The major purpose of these readings is to show that the concepts and requirements for the design of jobs have changed in recent years. The editors' introduction provides a framework for the job design area.

Contents

Part One: Evolution of Job Designs in Industrial Society
1. On the Economy of Machinery and Manufactures,
   Charles Babbage (1835)
2. The Principles of Scientific Management, Frederick
   W. Taylor (1911)
3. Three Technologies: Size, Measurement, Hierarchy,
   Daniel Bell (1956)
4. Operating Units, Robert Boguslaw (1965)
5. An Historical Theory in the Evolution of Industrial
   Skills, Alain Touraine (1962)
Part Two: The Current Condition
6. Current Job Design Criteria, Louis E. Davis, Ralph
   R. Canter, and John Hoffman (1955)

Topics

Automation
Autonomy
Change Strategy
Human Assets Accounting
Individual-Organization Interface
Job Design
Job Enlargement

Job Enrichment
Management
Motivation
Role
Satisfaction
Sociotechnical Systems
Technology

Margulies, Newton. "Organizational Culture and Psychological Growth."
JOURNAL OF APPLIED BEHAVIORAL SCIENCE 5, no. 4 (1969): 491-508.

"The study reported here explores the degree in which 'sociotechnical systems architecture' influences individual psychological growth.
Its major hypothesis is that a specific organizational culture, defined in terms of a specific set of values, attitudes, and behavioral
norms, can contribute to the degree in which persons can actualize
themselves."

An experiment with four departments at Non-Linear Systems is reported. Two departments took part in changes consisting of "elimi-
nating the routine, standardized assembly line and creating small
cohesive workgroups as the basis for organization" and changing
attitudes in the direction of Theory Y. The remaining groups continued to function in the more typical assembly line manner.

A variety of data collection methods (interviews, observations,
special surveys, generally used surveys) were used to tap work
values, attitudes, behavioral norms, and psychological growth.

The data indicated a positive relationship between value-orientations
and self-actualization. "The more intrinsic the value-orientation,
the more psychological growth. For the department, the more
the environment can encourage intrinsic satisfaction, the more
likely can that environment facilitate psychological growth." Also,
the author found that "higher self-actualization groups do exhibit
more awareness of the interconnectedness between task achievement
and social need satisfaction." Additionally, "the behavior of the
more self-actualizing groups is less determined by formal structure,
formal role prescriptions, or by Formal Authority . . . the behavior
of SA [self-actualizing] individuals is determined more by internalized values than by Formal Authority or Group Ideology."

The authors suggest that "overspecialization need not be an inevitable consequence of mass production."

Topics

Attitude/Attitude Change
Environment
Group Processes
Individual Growth
Mass Production

Norms
Overspecialization
Self-Actualization
Sociotechnical Systems
Values

Trist, E[ric].L. "On Socio-technical Systems." In THE PLANNING OF CHANGE, edited by Warren G. Bennis, Kenneth D. Benne, and Robert Chin, pp. 269-82. New York: Holt, Rinehart and Winston, 1969.

Trist states that a shift has occurred away from thinking of organizations as closed social systems and toward a view based on open-systems thinking, emphasizing the fit between the social and technical systems.

One result of this newer approach is a notion that group autonomy should not be maximized in all productive settings. The author suggests that there is an optimal level of autonomy determined by the requirements of the technological system.

Topics

Autonomy
Closed-System
Environment
Leadership
Management

Open-System
Organization Goal/Task
Sociotechnical Systems
Supervision
Technology

SURVEY-GUIDED DEVELOPMENT

Bowers, David G., and Franklin, Jerome L. SURVEY-GUIDED DEVELOPMENT I: DATA BASED ORGANIZATIONAL CHANGE. La Jolla, California: University Associates, 1977.

This volume describes a framework for organization development based on "a body of scientific knowledge concerning change theory and practice which (a) employs interpersonal process consultation skills but is not limited to them; (b) uses survey feedback but is much more than that, and (c) views organizational theory as a necessary companion to any organizational change effort" (p. ii).

Contents

Chapter 1: Prologue
Chapter 2: The Organization as a Social System
Chapter 3: The Nature of Change
Chapter 4: Systemic Diagnosis
Chapter 5: The Role of the Change Agent
Chapter 6: Survey Feedback
Chapter 7: The Evaluation of System Interventions
Chapter 8: Past Evidence, Present Practices, and Future Needs

Topics

Change Agent
Change Strategy
Change Technology
Diagnosis/Evaluation

Feedback
Survey Feedback
Survey-Guided Development
Survey of Organizations

129

_____. "Survey-guided Development". Using Human Resources Measurement in Organizational Change." JOURNAL OF CONTEMPORARY BUSINESS 1, no. 3 (1972): 43-55.

The authors present a description, together with the rationale and assumptions underlying an approach to improving organizational functioning based on the use of survey measurement. They use surveys as the basic measurement tool for diagnosing organizational functioning, including system properties of organizations; providing information that serves as a basis for the feedback process; and assessing changes produced by attempts aimed at improving organizational functioning.

In addition to providing a model of survey-guided development, the authors describe the change-agent role and the motivating processes inherent in this approach to organizational improvement.

Topics

Change Agent   Measurement
Change Goals   Motivation
Change Processes   Survey Feedback
Change Strategy   Survey-Guided Development
Diagnosis/Evaluation   System Approach
Feedback   Therapy
Human Organization

Hausser, Doris L.; Pecorella, Patricia A.; and Wissler, Anne L. SURVEY-GUIDED DEVELOPMENT II: A MANUAL FOR CONSULTANTS. La Jolla, California: University Associates, 1977.

This volume provides a thorough and detailed description of the consultant's role in effectively utilizing information gathered from organizational members as the basis of OD projects. Included are sections describing how questionnaire data can be gathered, evaluated, and fed back to respondents and system managers for the purpose of facilitating problem identification and problem-solving activities at both work group and organization-wide levels.

Contents

Section I: Theory and Measurement in Survey-Guided Development
    Module 1:   What is Survey-Guided Development?
    Module 2:   Using a Standardized Questionnaire: The
                Survey of Organizations
Section II: Activities and Concepts at the Work Group Level
    Module 3:   Understanding Work Group Data and Pre-
                paring Data Displays
    Module 4:   Meeting With Work Group Supervisor
    Module 5:   Work Group Feedback Meeting
Section III: Activities and Concepts at the Systemic Level
    Module 6:   Understanding and Presenting Systemic Data
    Module 7:   Identifying Systemic Problems
    Module 8:   Solving Systemic Problems

Section IV: Consultant Interventions
Module 9: Key Phrase Index: Consultant Skills and
Information

Topics

Change Agent	Group Processes
Change Strategy	Problem Solving
Consultant	Survey Feedback
Data Collection	Survey-Guided Development
Diagnosis/Evaluation	Survey of Organizations
Feedback	Work Group

TEAM BUILDING

Beckhard, Richard. "Optimizing Team-building Efforts." JOURNAL OF CON-
TEMPORARY BUSINESS 1, no. 3 (1972): 23-32.

Four general purposes (other than sharing information) are suggested
for group meetings: establishing goals or priorities, analyzing and
distributing the work, examining how the group works, and examining the relationships among the group members as they work.

Beckhard notes that consultants and managers tend to rank-order
these purposes differently in terms of importance. This situation
is the cause of misused energy in team-building efforts. The proposed solution is to sort out the rank-orderings and select a single
primary purpose. It is the responsibility of the team leader to
select this purpose and the responsibility of the third-party consultant to facilitate the work within the limits of that purpose.

Topics

Consultant	Team Building/Development
Leadership	Third Party

Crockett, William J. "Team Building--One Approach to Organizational Development." JOURNAL OF APPLIED BEHAVIORAL SCIENCE 6, no. 3 (1970):
291-306.

The supervisor of a work group in the U.S. Department of State
describes experiences and feelings during a two-day team-building
meeting.

The event focused on the work relationships within a group of
eleven persons. Data which have been previously gathered through
interviews served as the basis for the meeting.

The author concludes from the experience that team building is a
useful activity and that the Theory Y style of management is a
"tough-minded" approach.

Development Strategies and Techniques

Topics

Change Technology   Team Building/Development
Feedback   Theory Y
Management

Davis, Sheldon A. "Building More Effective Teams." INNOVATION 15
(1970): 32-41.

Davis distinguishes between team building and T-groups. T-groups
are temporary and have as their main goal individual learning.
Team building, in contrast, is described as "introspection among
a group of people who work together more or less continuously."

For team building to be effective, three elements are necessary:
time, participation by all members of the team, and a consultant
who is not a complete stranger to the group.

The consultant strives for two things in team building: (1) getting
the team members to really hear each other and to understand the
issues in a nondefensive way and (2) achieving a realization on
the part of team members that there are alternatives to the present
way of functioning.

Topics

Change Agent   Group Processes
Consultant   Team Building/Development
Group Development   T-Group

Friedlander, Frank. "The Impact of Organizational Training Laboratories upon
the Effectiveness and Interaction of Ongoing Work Groups." PERSONNEL
PSYCHOLOGY 20 (1967): 289-307.

Four work groups participated in organizational training laboratories
and eight were used as comparison groups.

Improvements were sought in six dimensions: group effectiveness, approach to vs. withdrawal from the leader, mutual influence, personal involvement and participation, intragroup trust vs. intragroup
competitiveness, and general evaluation of meetings.

The Group Behavior Inventory given before training and six months
after training was used to assess changes in the four experimental
groups. The Inventory was given at two times, separated by a six
month period, for the comparison groups.

"Significant changes occurred in training groups in the following
three dimensions: group effectiveness, mutual influence, and personal involvement. No significant changes occurred in leader ap-
proachability, intragroup trust, or in the evaluation of group meetings," the author notes.

The author concludes that "significant improvements in effectiveness and inter-action processes of work groups do occur as a result of participation in organizational training laboratories. These improvements take place in areas which are of direct personal and organizational relevance to members of the ongoing work groups and endure for a period of at least six months beyond the training experience."

This article reports one aspect of a study carried out with twelve family work groups from a 6,000 member R&D facility of the armed services. (See also Friedlander, pp. 61 and 65.)

Topics

Competition	Leadership
Durability of Training	Organizational Training
Group Behavior Inventory	Laboratory
Group Development	Participation
Group Effectiveness	Problem Solving
Influence	Trust

Gibb, Jack R. "TORI Theory: Consultantless Team-building." JOURNAL OF CONTEMPORARY BUSINESS 1, no. 3 (1972): 33-41.

"TORI theory is a view of social systems that is derived from both laboratory experimentation and field research." Gibb presents a statement of TORI theory as it applied to the development of business organizations along with a description of consultantless team-building programs and a summary of results from such programs.

Results indicate such programs are judged by participants to be more useful than those planned and conducted by consultants; when the focus is on operating problems, team effectiveness is improved better than when the focus is on process and personal issues; managers gain an increased appreciation for their own abilities to influence the system through such programs.

Topics

Consultant	Team Building/Development
Laboratory Training	TORI

OTHERS

Harvey, Jerry B., and Boettger, C. Russell. "Improving Communication within a Managerial Workshop." JOURNAL OF APPLIED BEHAVIORAL SCIENCE 7, no. 2 (1971): 164-80.

The authors describe a communications exercise carried out within the context of an ongoing organization development program. The participants were fifteen division directors and a vice-president who was their superior.

Preparation for the exercise included interviews with each of the sixteen persons involved; summarizing results of the interviews and identifying major problem areas--the areas isolated for this exercise were communications among the division directors and between the division directors and the vice president; and feeding back the interview data to the group of sixteen.

The actual three-hour experiment involved sharing perceptions around the meaning, priority, and action implications of four selected memos.

A subsequent evaluation of the experiment included five kinds of data: (1) generalized learnings (e.g., norms, criteria for assigning priorities); (2) quantitative data (i.e., number of memos sent by the vice president over time); (3) reactions of subordinates; (4) reactions of the vice president; and (5) potential savings (e.g., monetary value of time saved). From these data sources the authors concluded "that application of an experienced-based change intervention did produce results which could be measured with both soft (attitudinal) and hard (production or monetary) measures."

Topics

Communications
Diagnosis/Evaluation
Feedback

Laboratory Approach
Team Building/Development
Trust

Morton, R.B., and Bass, B[ernard].M. "The Organizational Training Laboratory." TRAINING DIRECTORS JOURNAL 18, no. 10 (1964): 2-18.

The authors describe a technique used to allow trainees to learn through group process and to help build a climate that supports learning.

The Organizational Training Laboratory is composed of intact work groups and includes a week of training about intragroup and intergroup processes and three days devoted to the application of these learnings to actual organizational problems.

A study based on self-reports indicated that participants showed favorable attitudes toward the technique. Ninety-seven participants reported 359 critical incidents showing "improved working relations (38 percent), personal improvement (35 percent), conflict reduction (6 percent), difficulties in applying [the] training (17 percent) and unfavorable comments (1 percent)."

Topics

Conflict/Conflict Resolution
Group Processes
Intergroup Processes

Organizational Training
Laboratory
Transfer of Training
Work Group

Section 3

CASE STUDIES

Each of the case studies contained within Section 3 focuses on a limited number or type of organization involved in development efforts. Together, these cases represent a variety of organizational types, including production-oriented business, health care, hotel, education, community, and government. The literature included in this section is characterized by in-depth descriptions, by organization development efforts involving a variety of activities or interventions, and by descriptions focusing on several important issues.

The most outstanding case study reported since the mid-1960s is probably the work by Marrow, Bowers, and Seashore (See p. 145). This book contains various strengths, particularly an interweaving of descriptive materials with careful empirical analyses. The descriptive materials are supplied by a number of principals in the OD activities, including the plant manager, researchers, the company president, and engineering and behavioral scientist consultants. Empirical analyses of various aspects of this effort explore the effects on attitudes, behaviors, and performance. The value of this case is further strengthened by a followup evaluation by Seashore and Bowers (See p. 148) assessing long-term effects of the OD effort.

Alschuler, Alfred. "Toward a Self-Renewing School." JOURNAL OF APPLIED BEHAVIORAL SCIENCE 8, no. 5 (1972): 577-600.

This study describes the implementation of psychological curricula in a community college through OD strategies. An analysis of events leading to and contributing to the changes suggests that three factors are necessary for sustained change: a high level of system readiness prior to any organizational development effort; a combined effort of organizational development and psychological education; and the continuous leadership of key individuals within the organization before, during, and after the participation of outside change agents.

Topics

Achievement Motivation	Change Technology
Change Agent	Education
Change Processes	Motivation
Change Strategy	Motivation Training

135

Beckhard, Richard. "An Organization Improvement Program in a Decentralized Organization." JOURNAL OF APPLIED BEHAVIORAL SCIENCE 2, no. 1 (1966): 3-25

Beckhard reports on a five-year project in an organization operating twenty-six hotel properties, during which the following activities took place: interviews; three-day offsite feedback meetings; follow-up meetings; three meetings held six months apart for feedback with hotel managers and their teams; problem-solving conferences; training laboratory for president, two vice-presidents, several hotel general managers, and two or three staff directors; two-day planning conference to look at progress toward management by objectives or Theory Y; management school to provide cognitive awareness regarding the managers' own behavior, concepts relevant to organizational development, and management by objectives; technical seminars to broaden technical skills; team training for new hotels; operations improvement committees; and a cost reduction program.

No clear measures of change were available; however, improvements in profits, turnover, performance (costs related to sales), and crisis management were reported.

Included in the article are several general notes on the phases and necessary conditions for effective planned change. In addition, Beckhard notes that priorities should be set among the various types of changes (attitudes, skills, climate) that can be sought.

Topics

Attitude/Attitude Change	Laboratory Training
Change Phases	Management by Objectives
Climate	Problem Solving
Feedback	Skill
Interview	Team Building/Development

Bowers, David G. "Three Studies in Change: An Account of Data-based Organizational Development Activities in Three Continuous Process Firms." Technical Report to the Office of Naval Research, Arlington, Va., 1969. (Available from Defense Documentation Center, Cameron Station, Alexandria, Va.)

Change programs employing a variety of techniques, mainly survey feedback, the Managerial Grid, and laboratory-type activities, are described.

Implications drawn from the study include the following: "Positive sanction of top management is apparently necessary for the success of the program, either by its personal commitment and involvement, by its official power, or, at the very least by its willingness not to undercut the program. To the extent that these data indicate greater or less effectiveness of any particular form of sanction, they suggest that there is more to be gained by sanctioning through the power of office than by personal commitment alone . . . the findings suggest that a change program, to be effective, must be geared into the working system of the organization."

Topics

Change Forces	Managerial Grid
Change Strategy	Survey Feedback
Laboratory Training	

Bowers, David G., and Seashore, Stanley E. "Changing the Structure and Functioning of an Organization." In ORGANIZATIONAL EXPERIMENTS: LABORATORY AND FIELD RESEARCH, edited by William M. Evan, pp. 185-201. New York: Harper & Row, 1971.

This chapter describes a multifaceted change effort in a large packaging materials firm. The study undertaken in conjunction with the change project defined several propositions concerning organizational improvement. The authors conclude that an organization is likely to achieve its purposes better if there is an emphasis on the work group, rather than exclusively on the individual, as the unit supervised; if there is a high rate of interaction and mutual influence among work group members; if there is a high degree of participation in decision making and control activities in the lower echelons of the organization; and if supervisors are highly supportive to subordinates.

"In general, there is evidence supporting the validity of the propositions embodied in the study design, but this evidence is not so strong and well-controlled from confounding influences as to be conclusive."

Topics

Change Strategy	Influence
Control	Participation
Decision Making	Support
Group Processes	Work Group

Bragg, J.E., and Andrews, I.R. "Participative Decision Making: An Experimental Study in a Hospital." JOURNAL OF APPLIED BEHAVIORAL SCIENCE 9, no. 6 (1973): 727-35.

An eighteen-month study of participative decision making in a hospital laundry with thirty-two unionized workers resulted in improved attitudes, reduced absence rates, and increased productivity. Contrasts with comparison groups from two other hospital laundries and the overall hospital indicated differences which were "significant practically as well as statistically" (p. 727). Among the other positive results was a cost savings of $1,000 per employee per year.

Topics

| Absence | Change Strategy |
| Attitude/Attitude Change | Decision Making |

Durability of Change	Productivity
Participation	Resistance to Change
Performance	Unfreezing

Brown, L. Dave. "'Research Action': Organizational Feedback, Understanding, and Change." JOURNAL OF APPLIED BEHAVIORAL SCIENCE 8, no. 6 (1972): 697-711.

The author stresses a mutual exchange of information between researchers and clients as a critical element for diagnosing and affecting change in a system. A case study of organizational diagnosis and feedback in a school leads to the following conclusion: "Information sharing between investigator and respondent affects both the quality of relationship between them and the adequacy of the diagnosis."

An interactive model is presented suggesting that "the respondent's action is contingent on . . . his diagnosis of the investigator, which is based in turn on . . . the investigator's actions . . . and his diagnostic activities. . . . " Action and research are viewed as being potentially synergistic in some situations, even though they may be competitive activities in other situations.

Topics

Action Research	Self-Perception Questionnaire
Diagnosis/Evaluation	Time Series Questionnaire
Feedback	

Brown, L. Dave; Aram, John D.; and Bachner, David J. "Interorganizational Information Sharing: A Successful Intervention that Failed." JOURNAL OF APPLIED BEHAVIORAL SCIENCE 10, no. 4 (1974): 533-54.

The authors describe interventions with a consortium of seven schools of theology aimed at increasing "the amount and accuracy of information shared by participant organizations"; increasing organizational consensus; and decreasing interorganizational problems of coordination. The interventions, which consisted of campus visits for diagnostic purposes and a management skills workshop, attained the first goal but failed to accomplish the second two. Workshop participation increased coordination problems, rather than decreased them.

Other observations from this study indicated that "the diagnostic process may have had the unplanned effect of increasing the perceived importance of the issues under investigation" and "third parties are likely to be ineffectual if they are seen as another principal rather than as a neutral."

Topics

Change Strategy	Education/Schools
Consensus	Interorganizational
Consultant	Problem Solving
Cooperation	Third Party

Burns, Tom, and Stalker, G.M. THE MANAGEMENT OF INNOVATION. London: Tavistock, 1961. 269 p.

In the framework of "mechanistic" and "organic" systems, the authors describe changes in the electronics industry. The studies reviewed concentrate on "the management difficulties which seemed peculiar to firms engaged in rapid technical progress, and the particular problem of getting laboratory groups on the one hand (research--development--design) to work effectively with production and sales groups on the other."

The authors conclude that: "Technical progress and organizational development are aspects of one and the same trend in human affairs; and the persons who work to make these processes actual are also their victims.

"As the rate of change increases in the technical field, so does the number of occasions which demand quick and effective interpretation between people working in different parts of the system. As the rate of change increases in the market field, so does the need to multiply the points of contact between the concern and the markets it wishes to explore and develop.

"The shift from mechanistic to organic procedures, therefore, makes considerable demands on individual members of an organization. In general terms, they are required to surrender the same determinacy of a contractual relationship with the firm for one in which their obligations are far less limited, to replace a view of the firm as an impersonal, immutable boss by one which regards it as something kept in being by the sustained creative activity of themselves and other members, to cease being 'nine-to-fivers' and turn 'professionals.'"

Topics

Innovation   Organic Systems
Mechanistic Systems   Technology

Culbert, Samuel A. "Using Research to Guide an Organization Development Project." JOURNAL OF APPLIED BEHAVIORAL SCIENCE 8, no. 2 (1972): 203-36.

A case study is presented which describes how research was used in an organization development effort to help the clients move from a focus on specific problems to a focus on systemwide issues.

The case includes an examination of the differences in problem-solving perspectives held by OD consultants and their clients; a description of the specific consultant and client differences in each instance and the research and training design worked out to mediate between them; a report on how research data were first analyzed to address questions raised at the beginning of the study and then reanalyzed to suggest directions for future action and inquiry; and a discussion of some generalizable lessons, derived from the case, for experimenting with change during times of organizational crisis.

Topics

Attitude Toward Renewal Questionnaire	Do's and Dont's Questionnaire
Change Agent	Personal Relations Survey
Change Strategy	Problem Solving
Conflict/Conflict Resolution	Sensitivity Training
Consultation	T-Group
Data Collection	Who Do You Know? Questionnaire
Diagnosis/Evaluation	Who Knows You? Questionnaire

Dowling, William F. "The Corning Approach to Organization Development." ORGANIZATIONAL DYNAMICS 3 (Spring 1975): 16-34.

Generalizations concerning organization development are derived from an overview of some of the experiences at Corning Glass Works Corporation. Six primary issues serve as a focus for the article: entry, bottom-up or top-down sponsorship, effective technology, ownership, feedback, and evaluation. A major theme is that "effectiveness [in OD efforts] depends on the proper fit between tools or technology and the particular problem" (p. 17).

Topics

Absenteeism	Feedback
Attitude/Attitude Change	Managerial Grid
Behavior Change	Organizational Climate
Change Agent	Problem Solving
Change Strategy	Process Consultation
Change Technology	Resistance
Commitment	Satisfaction
Consultant	Structure
Diagnosis/Evaluation	Team Building
Entry	T-Group
Evaluation	Values

Dyer, William G., et al. "A Laboratory-Consultation Model for Organizational Change." JOURNAL OF APPLIED BEHAVIORAL SCIENCE 6, no. 2 (1970): 211-27.

The authors offer a case study of an organizational development effort stressing problems of entry and transfer. The project attempted to optimize both entry methods and transfer activities by a single development approach. This approach uses laboratory training to build a consulting relationship between internal consultants and their operating managers in an industrial organization.

The design included four parts: laboratory training as an initiating vehicle; the use of internal Trainer-Consultants; the use of data collection and feedback; and a single management and organizational conceptual framework.

"Initial results from back-home application within the organization indicate that these design features have reduced the entry and transfer problems experienced in utilizing laboratory learnings in organization development. However, certain problems still exist in transfer of learning, namely: uneven skill on the part of the managers to implement laboratory learnings, some lack of skill on the part of the Trainer-Consultants to intervene effectively, and the existence of certain organization conditions that do not support change," the authors write.

Topics

Change Agent   Laboratory Training
Consultation   Resistance to Change
Data Collection   Skill
Entry   Trainer
Feedback   Transfer of Training
Intervention

French, John R.P., Jr.; Israel, Joachim; and Aas, Dagfinn. "An Experiment on Participation in a Norwegian Factory." HUMAN RELATIONS 13, no. 1 (1960): 3-10.

This report replicates a previous study on participation and produc-tion, management-worker relations, and job satisfaction.

There was no difference between the experimental and control groups in the level of production. "With respect to worker-management relations, there was support for the hypothesis that the effects of participation as they consider legitimate. There was equal support for the hypothesis that the effects of participation increase with decreasing resistance to the participation methods," the authors discovered.

Topics

Participation   Satisfaction
Resistance to Change

Giacquinta, Joseph B.; London, Herbert I.; and Shigaki, Irene S. "Imple-menting Organizational Changes in Urban Schools: The Case of Paraprofession-als." JOURNAL OF APPLIED BEHAVIORAL SCIENCE 9, no. 4 (1973): 469-83.

Paraprofessionals, teachers, and school administrators provided data for a study of factors related to the successful implementation of organizational innovations. Results indicated that "paraprofessional clarity, willingness, ability, resources, and school compatibility . . were predictive of differences in the implementation of the pro-grams" (p. 469).

Topics

Implementation Questionnaire   Role
Innovation   Role Definition Questionnaire

Greenblatt, Milton; Sharaf, Myron R.; and Stone, Evelyn M. DYNAMICS OF INSTITUTIONAL CHANGE: THE HOSPITAL IN TRANSITION. Pittsburgh: University of Pittsburgh Press, 1971. 260 p.

This case study concerning a large mental hospital documents "administrative issues involved in trying to make a complex public facility more alive, more flexible, and more responsive to the people it serves" (p. xviii). The book is primarily focused on the problems hampering change and the gains and losses of one or another strategy of change.

Contents

Part I: Concept and Techniques of Change
  1. Within the Institution
  2. The Institution and the Community
  3. Philosophy of Treatment: Some Issues and Difficulties
  4. Decentralization Through Unitization
Part II: Special Services
  5. The Adolescent Consultation Service
  6. The Rehabilitation Service
  7. Volunteers
Part III: Education and Research
  8. Psychiatric Education by Myron R. Sharaf
  9. Research by Milton Greenblatt
Epilogue by Milton Greenblatt

Topics

Change Strategy   Public Service Organizations
Decentralization   Resistance to Change
Leadership

Hautaluoma, Jacob E., and Gavin, James F. "Effects of Organizational Diagnosis and Intervention on Blue-Collar 'Blues.'" JOURNAL OF APPLIED BEHAVIORAL SCIENCE 11, no. 4 (1975): 475-96.

An OD project was initiated to counteract high turnover among blue-collar employees in a small manufacturing company. Diagnosis was based on interviews and questionnaire data gathered from all employees. Interventions included feedback, supervisory skills training, and process observation.

Results of these activities showed positive effects on turnover, absenteeism, and attitudes. The authors point out that despite a lack of attention given to the lowest level employees, the interventions apparently had positive impacts resulting in a reduction of "blue-collar blues."

Topics

Absenteeism	Feedback
Attitude/Attitude Change	Interview
Change Strategy	Job Descriptive Index
Climate	Skill Training
Consultant	Survey Feedback
Diagnosis/Evaluation	Team Building/Development
Durability of Change	Turnover

Kegan, Daniel L., and Rubenstein, Albert H. "Trust, Effectiveness, and Organizational Development: A Field Study in R & D." JOURNAL OF APPLIED BEHAVIORAL SCIENCE 9, no. 4 (1973): 498-513.

Individuals in nine research and development groups from three organizations provided the basis for investigating trust among group members. Results indicated "the more an individual trusts his workgroup and the more he generally trusts others with whom he interacts during his work, the greater will be his self-actualization; . . . a 'proper' organizational development program will increase an individual's feelings of trust toward his own group and toward others, while maintaining awareness of the demands of his tasks. A third hypothesis received mixed support: the more the members of a group trust that group, and the more they generally trust others with whom they interact during their work, the more effective the group will be in its goal accomplishment" (p. 498).

Topics

Climate	Process Consultation
Communications	Self-Actualization
Cousins Laboratory	Sensitivity Training
Defensiveness	Team Building/Development
Encounter Group	Trust
Human Relations Training	
Openness	

Kimberly, John R., and Nielsen, Warren R. "Organization Development and Change in Organizational Performance." ADMINISTRATIVE SCIENCE QUARTERLY 20, no. 2 (1975): 191-206.

An OD effort in a 2,800 member automotive plant of a large corporation is the focus for an evaluation of the consequences of such projects. The change program included seven stages: initial diagnosis (interviews, group meetings, change effort designing); team skills training; data collection (two questionnaires); data confrontation (problem identification and prioritization); action planning (development of recommendations for change); team building; and intergroup building.

Several positive results were indicated as outcomes from the OD activities. Included were "improved organizational performance, as well as positive change in attitudes and perceptions, . . . [and]

changes in behavior, which were reflected, in turn, in changes in organizational performance." Beyond this "perceptions of organizationally anchored phenomena . . . improved; . . . production variance decreased, rates of quality increased, variance in quality decreased, and profits increased" (p. 203).

Topics

Attitude/Attitude Change   Quality
Performance

Levin, Gilbert, and Stein, David D. "System Intervention in a School-Community Conflict." JOURNAL OF APPLIED BEHAVIORAL SCIENCE 6, no. 3 (1970): 337-52.

This case describes an exercise designed to bring together several parties in a school-community conflict to "generate major educational concerns" and presumably to improve relationships among the participants. The intervention was a forum designed by staff from a community mental health center responding to pressures from staff members and interested parties in the conflict. The forum featured a warm-up period, permitting significant group-building interaction, and the translation of a laboratory intergroup exercise into a format that works in a community conflict situation.

Topics

Change Strategy   Group Cohesiveness
Community Mental Health Center   Intergroup Laboratory
Conflict/Conflict Resolution   School

Luke, Robert A., Jr., et al. "A Structural Approach to Organizational Change." JOURNAL OF APPLIED BEHAVIORAL SCIENCE 9, no. 5 (1973): 611-35.

A case study explains the process by which the management--attitudes, behavior, and structures--of a retail food organization underwent a change from closed control of employees to a form of training and consultation for employees. "Measured by indices of profit and productivity, as well as indices of employee attitude and morale, the project was successful" (p. 611). Notable aspects of this project were the structural nature of the change and the "architect" as contrasted with the more usual "trainer-intervenor" nature of the consultant's activities.

Topics

Administrative Structure   Control
Attitude/Attitude Change   Durability of Change
Authority   Management Training/Development
Autonomy   Performance
Behavior Change   Productivity
Change Strategy   Risk/Risk-Taking
Consultation   Sensitivity Training
                                Team Building/Development

McMillan, Charles B. "Organizational Change in Schools: Bedford-Stuyvesant." JOURNAL OF APPLIED BEHAVIORAL SCIENCE 11, no. 4 (1975): 437-53.

Personal interviews and project data serve as the basis for reconstructing a two-year intervention whose goal was to improve a junior high school. The intervenors set out to increase community involvement and effect broad social change in education, relying on two generally accepted theories of planned organizational change: subordinate participation in decision making and the importance of leadership behavior as exhibited by the change agent.

"The study concludes that organizational change theories--if used wisely--would be suitable for reaching the goals of improved teaching-learning sought for the schools, but would not be useful in fundamentally increasing community participation or using schools to effect social change--goals that are obstructed by a larger political reality" (p. 437).

Topics

Change Strategy   Participation
Commitment   Problem Solving
Diagnosis/Evaluation

Marrow, Alfred J. "Managerial Revolution in the State Department." PERSONNEL 43, no. 6 (1966): 8-18.

Marrow outlines an organizational development effort that brought together many outside resources to facilitate efforts in management by objectives, laboratory training, team building, and problem solving.

Topics

Change Strategy   Problem Solving
Laboratory Training   Team Building/Development
Management by Objectives

Marrow, Alfred J.; Bowers, David G.; and Seashore, Stanley E. MANAGEMENT BY PARTICIPATION. New York: Harper & Row, 1967. 264 p.

This book reports an extensive study of a multifaceted change effort. The change effort involved the resources of managers, engineers, and behavioral scientists. This volume reports the effort and its outcomes from several points of view.

Assessments of the effects of various aspects of the effort were conducted by persons not directly involved in implementing the changes. Various portions of the total gains attributed to the effort were determined to be related to specific changes. "The earnings development program with individual operators was the most potent of the steps undertaken, contributing perhaps 11 percentage of the total gain of 30 points. Next in order of influence were the weeding out of low earners . . . and the provision of training for supervisors and staff in interpersonal relations, each contribution about 5 percentage points to the total gain. The group consultation and problem resolution program with operators appears to have contributed about 3 percentage points. The balance of 6 percentage points can be viewed as arising from miscellaneous sources or from the combination of the several program elements."

(See also Seashore and Bowers, below, for a followup report).

Contents

Part One: The Weldon Company, 1962.

Contributing Authors

Bowers, D.G.	Marrow, A.J.	Roberts, E.E.
Brooks, C.	Nelson, J.R.	Seashore, S.E.
David, G.	Pearse, R.F.	Smith, J.F.
Kornbluh, H.		

Topics

Attitude/Attitude Change	Interpersonal Processes
Change Processes	Management
Change Strategy	Motivation
Communications	Performance
Earnings Development Program	Problem Solving
Feedback	Satisfaction
Human Organization	Technological Change
	Trust

Miller, Eric J. "Socio-Technical Systems in Weaving, 1953-1970: A Followup Study." HUMAN RELATIONS 28, no. 4 (1975): 349-86.

This is a followup report of changes established in nonautomatic

and automatic weaving operations in India. The primary change
established semi-autonomous work groups.

Results indicated that in the nonautomatic setting "the work organization and levels of performance had remained virtually unchanged
over the 16 years" while benefits in the automatic setting had
largely disappeared (p. 349).

Topics

Attitude/Attitude Change   Performance
Change Strategy   Sociotechnical Systems
Durability of Change   Structural Change
Group Process

Nadler, David A., and Pecorella, Patricia A. "Differential Effects of Multiple
Interventions in an Organization." JOURNAL OF APPLIED BEHAVIORAL SCI-
ENCE 11, no. 3 (1975): 348-66.

The authors evaluate effects of a multi-year change program involving several interventions by using survey and clinical data, and
discover differential outcomes among three different levels of hierarchy.

Interventions included management development, team building,
survey feedback, and adjustments in the compensation system. The
authors note that this collection of interventions were not well
integrated in their application.

Three major patterns were identified from the study: (1) in general,
the interventions impacted positively on the line production workers
but did not result in high levels of satisfaction with work tasks
themselves. (2) Dissatisfaction emerged for middle-level employees
(e.g., supervisory and technical employees). (3) Top and middle-
level managers exhibited moderate dissatisfaction, apparently caused
by low goal clarity, which probably predated the intervention work.
According to these authors, the results "indicate that the possibility
exists for mixed effects in otherwise successful change programs.
There are also indications that with a less integrated and coordi-
nated collection of interventions, the risk of unintended or unanticipated differential effects becomes greater" (p. 363).

Topics

Autonomy   Measurement
Change Strategy   Participation
Compensation   Satisfaction
Decision Making   Survey Feedback
Goals (Individual/Organizational)   Survey of Organizations
Hierarchy   Task
Management Training/Development   Team Building/Development

Peek, Barbara, ed. AN ACTION RESEARCH PROGRAM FOR ORGANIZA-
TIONAL IMPROVEMENT. Ann Arbor, Mich.: Foundation for Research on

Case Studies

Human Behavior, 1960. 71 p.

Peek describes work done at Esso Standard Oil Company. Among
the development techniques discussed are offsite management conferences, development groups, data feedback, and laboratory training.

The elements of an action research model are presented, as well
as information regarding intergroup competition.

Contributing Authors

Blake, R.R.   Katzell, R.A.   Shepard, H.A.
Horwitz, M.   Kolb, H.D.

Topics

Action Research   Intergroup Processes
Competition   Laboratory Training
Feedback   Management Conference

Seashore, Stanley E., and Bowers, David G. "The Durability of Organizational Change." AMERICAN PSYCHOLOGIST 25, no. 3 (1970): 227-33.

The authors report on a 1969 survey used to evaluate the long-
term effects of an earlier change effort (Marrow, Bowers, and Seashore, 1967, above). Lasting changes were found.

Three possible explanations are offered to account for the durability
of the changes: the breadth of the changes across domains (psychological, organizational, technical); legitimization of concern
about organizational process; and inherent merit of the participative
organizational model.

Topics

Change Processes   Durability of Change
Change Strategy   Participation

Trist, Eric L., and Bamforth, R. "Some Social and Psychological Consequences
of the Long Wall Method of Coal-getting." HUMAN RELATIONS 4, no. 1
(1951): 3-38.

A case is reported in which increases in productivity of coal miners
is partially attributed to increases in group-relatedness after changes
in mining techniques.

Topics

Group Processes   Sociotechnical Systems

Winn, Alexander. "Social Change in Industry: From Insight to Implementation."
JOURNAL OF APPLIED BEHAVIORAL SCIENCE 2, no. 2 (1966): 170-83.

The author traces thirty years of change efforts in a major company, Alcan. The sequence of change efforts includes lectures

(in the 1940s), case studies and some role playing (in the 1950s), T-groups (in the 1960s), and family and interface (intergroup) laboratories.

Winn emphasizes the nature of laboratory training and the comparative advantages and inherent risks in using each type described.

Topics

Commitment	Laboratory Training
Confrontation	Lecture
Family Laboratory	Role Playing
Interface Laboratory	T-Group
Intergroup Laboratory	Transfer of Training

Zand, Dale [E.]; Steele, Fred [I.]; and Zalkind, Sheldon. "The Impact of an Organization Development Program on Perceptions of Interpersonal, Group and Organization Functioning." JOURNAL OF APPLIED BEHAVIORAL SCIENCE 5, no. 3 (1969): 393-410.

The authors describe a study conducted to evaluate the effects of participation in five-day cousins laboratories on 120 middle-level managers. The managers were members of a large research and engineering company that had a development program including stranger laboratory experiences for the president and vice-presidents, team development sessions, consultation from outside consultants, and cousins laboratories.

Four self-reported, paper-and-pencil questionnaire instruments were used to gather data at three points in time: before the laboratory experience, after the laboratory experience, and one year after the beginning of the effort.

The results indicate "(1) The immediate effect of attending a relatively unstructured laboratory seemed to be to alter the standards a participant used to evaluate various dimensions of his relations with others. In particular, there were declines in perceptions of one's trust of others, openness in communication, seeking and accepting of help, and receptivity of one's superior to the ideas of others which could be attributed to the use of more stringent standards of behavior. (2) A year later there were significant increases (for participants compared with non-participants) in perceptions of the extent to which managers were facing up to conflicts and were seeking help. (3) Ratings by other members in the same T-Group of one's behavior and learning at the laboratory seem to be useful as a predictor of the likelihood that a manager will be involved in follow-up activities with his work team. (4) [Participants] held what might be called 'socially correct' attitudes to start with, and these were not affected by the program."

Topics

Attitude/Attitude Change	Conflict/Conflict Resolution
Communications	Cousins Laboratory

Durability of Training
Interpersonal Processes
Laboratory Training
Management
Openness

Perception
Stranger Laboratory
Team Building/Development
Transfer of Training

Appendix A

PERIODICAL ADDRESSES

Administrative Science Quarterly
Graduate School of Business and
    Public Administration
Cornell University
Ithaca, N.Y.   14850

American Psychologist
American Psychological Association
1200 Seventeenth Street, N.W.
Washington, D.C.   20036

California Management Review
350 Barrows Hall
School of Business
University of California
Berkeley, Calif.   94720

Harvard Business Review
Graduate School of Business
    Administration
Harvard University
Boston, Mass.   02163

Human Organization
Society for Applied Anthropology
Lafferty Hall
University of Kentucky
Lexington, Ky.   40506

Human Relations
Plenum Press
227 West Seventeenth Street
New York, N.Y.   10011

Industrial Relations Research
    Association
Social Science Building
Madison, Wis.   53706

Innovation
American Institutes for Research
Box 1113
Palo Alto, Calif.   94302

International Journal of Group
    Psychotherapy
(American Group Psychotherapy
    Association)
1865 Broadway, Twelfth Floor
New York, N.Y.   10023

Journal of Abnormal and Social
    Psychology
American Psychological Association
1200 Seventeenth Street, N.W.
Washington, D.C.   20036

Journal of Applied Behavioral Science
NTL Institute
P.O. Box 9155, Rosslyn Station
Arlington, Va.   22209

Journal of Applied Psychology
American Psychological Institute
1200 Seventeenth Street, N.W.
Washington, D.C.   20036

Journal of Applied Social Psychology
Scripta Publishing Corp.
1511 K Street, N.W.
Washington, D.C. 20005

Journal of Contemporary Business
Graduate School of Business
   Administration
University of Washington
Seattle, Wash. 98195

Journal of Management Studies
Basil Blackwell and Mott
108 Cowley Road
Oxford OX4 1JF
Great Britain

Journal of Social Issues
Society for the Psychological Study
   of Social Issues
Box 1248
Ann Arbor, Mich. 48106

Kansas Business Review
See Kansas Economic Indicators

Kansas Economic Indicators (formerly
   Kansas Business Review)
Wichita State University
Wichita, Kans. 67208

Management Accounting
National Association of Accountants
919 Third Avenue
New York, N.Y. 10022

National Industrial Conference Board
845 Third Avenue
New York, N.Y. 10022

NTL Institute
1815 North Fort Myer Drive
Arlington, Va. 22209

Organizational Dynamics
American Management Association
AMACOM
135 West Fiftieth Street
New York, N.Y. 10020

Personnel
American Management Association
135 West Fiftieth Street
New York, N.Y. 10020

Personnel Administration
Society for Personnel Administration
484 National Press Building
Fourteenth at F Street, N.W.
Washington, D.C. 20004

Personnel Psychology
Box 6965
College Station
Durham, N.C. 27708

Psychological Bulletin
American Psychological Association
1200 Seventeenth Street, N.W.
Washington, D.C. 20036

Psychological Review
American Psychological Association
1200 Seventeenth Street, N.W.
Washington, D.C. 20036

Psychology Today
Communications/Research/Machines
317 Fourteenth Street
Del Mar, Calif. 92014

Public Opinion Quarterly
(American Association for Public
   Opinion Research)
Columbia University
Journalism Building, Room 510
New York, N.Y. 10027

Public Personnel Management
International Personnel Management
   Association
1313 East Sixtieth Street
Chicago, Ill. 60637

Sloan Management Review
Massachusetts Institute of Technology
Fifty Memorial Drive
Cambridge, Mass. 02139

Training and Development Journal
American Society for Training and
    Development
313 Price Place
Box 5307
Madison, Wis.   53705

Appendix B

ADDRESSES OF BOOK PUBLISHERS

Addison-Wesley Publishers
Reading, Mass. 01867

American Management Association
AMACOM
135 West Fiftieth Street
New York, N.Y. 10020

Annual Reviews
4139 El Camino Way
Palo Alto, Calif. 94306

Brigham Young University Press
205 University Press Building
Provo, Utah 84602

Columbia University Press
440 West 110th Street
New York, N.Y. 10025

Foundation for Research on
  Human Behavior
P.O. Box 1248
Ann Arbor, Mich. 48106

Free Press
MacMillan & Co.
866 Third Avenue
New York, N.Y. 10022

Gulf Publishing Co.
P.O. Box 2608
Houston, Tex. 77001

Harcourt Brace Jovanovich
757 Third Avenue
New York, N.Y. 10017

Harper & Row Publishers
49 E. Thirty Street
New York, N.Y. 10016

Holt, Rinehart and Winston
Columbia Broadcasting System
383 Madison Avenue
New York, N.Y. 10017

Institute for Social Research
University of Michigan
426 Thompson Street
Ann Arbor, Mich. 48106

Richard D. Irwin
1818 Ridge Road
Homewood, Ill. 60430

McGraw-Hill Book Co.
330 W. Forty-second Street
New York, N.Y. 10036

Oxford University Press
200 Madison Avenue
New York, N.Y. 10016

National Press Books
850 Hanson Way
Palo Alto, Calif.

NTL Institute
1815 North Fort Myer Drive
Arlington, Va. 22209

F.T. Peacock Publishers
401 W. Irving Park Road
Itasca, Ill. 60143

Penguin Books
72 Fifth Avenue
New York, N.Y. 10011

Pitman Publishing
6 E. Forty-third Street
New York, N.Y.

Prentice-Hall
Englewood Cliffs, N.J. 07632

Rand McNally and Co.
Box 7600
Chicago, Ill. 60611

Scott, Foresman and Co.
1900 E. Lake Avenue
Glenview, Ill. 60025

Tavistock Publishers
11 New Fetter Lane
London, E.C. 4
Great Britain

University Associates Publishers
7596 Eads Avenue
La Jolla, Calif. 92037

University of Iowa Press
Center for Labor and Management
College of Business Administration
Iowa City, Iowa 52242

University of Massachusetts Press
P.O. Box 429
Amherst, Mass. 01002

University of Pittsburgh Press
127 N. Bellefield Avenue
Pittsburgh, Pa. 15213

Wadsworth Publishers
Belmont, Calif. 94002

West Publishing Co.
50 Kellogg Building
St. Paul, Minn. 55102

John Wiley & Sons
605 Third Avenue
New York, N.Y. 10016

AUTHOR INDEX

This index is alphabetized letter by letter. In addition to authors, it includes all editors, compilers, and translators cited in this text.

A

Aas, Dagfinn 141
Abramowitz, Stephen I. 109
Abrams, D.W. 10
Albanese, Robert 17, 47
Albers, Carl H. 53
Albertson, D.R. 49
Alderfer, Clayton P. 50, 54, 69, 83, 90
Allen, Vernon L. 115
Alper, S. William 84
Alschuler, Alfred 135
Anderson, James D. 49
Anderson, John W. 51, 52, 84, 90
Andrews, I.R. 137
Aplin, John C., Jr. 85
Aram, John D. 45, 63, 138
Argyris, Chris A. 1-3, 9, 17, 20, 23, 48, 51, 52, 54-55, 97-98, 108
Aronoff, Joel 120
Atkins, Stuart 9, 110

B

Babbage, Charles 126
Bachner, David J. 45, 138
Bamforth, R. 148
Barnes, Louis B. 17, 23, 35, 47, 48, 51, 52, 108

Barrett, Jon H. 24
Bartlett, Alton C. 46, 47
Bass, Bernard M. 98, 104, 108, 134
Bauer, R.A. 48
Baumgartel, Howard 85
Beach, David N. 53
Beak, Joel 32
Becker, H.S. 48
Beckhard, Richard 3, 9, 10, 17, 48, 51, 52, 81, 131, 136
Beer, Michael 25, 37
Bell, Cecil H., Jr. 33
Bell, Daniel 48, 126
Benedict, Barbara A. 70
Benne, Kenneth D. 17, 25, 30, 42, 45, 48, 59, 61, 64, 98, 116, 129
Bennis, Warren G. 4-5, 10, 17, 23, 25, 26, 30, 42, 45, 46, 47, 48, 60, 64, 98, 99, 101, 108, 114, 129
Bereiter, Carl 71
Berkowitz, L. 10
Berlew, David E. 109
Bessell, H. 108
Bigelow, R.C. 21
Biggane, James F. 127
Billel, Lester R. 99
Birnbaum, Max 25

TITLE INDEX

This index is alphatetized letter by letter.   Journals and titles of articles are not included.

SUBJECT INDEX

This index is alphabetized letter by letter. References are to page numbers.

O

Openness
Operations analysis 36
Opinion change 48, 56
Organic-adaptive 122
Organic research 3
Organic systems 34, 122, 129, 139
Organization
  development of 40, 44, 107
  effectiveness of 5, 14, 27, 31, 52, 55, 98
  entropy of 3
  forms of 59
  goal and task 27, 112, 129
  growth of 31, 44, 90
  health of 5, 31
  life of 40
  style of 109
Organizational climate. See Climate
Organizational crisis 32-33, 58-59
Organizational design 122
Organizational Training Laboratory 61, 65, 133-34
Overcompensation 117
Overspecialization 128

P

Participation 6, 11, 24, 47, 53, 57, 61, 73, 96, 112-13, 122, 125-26, 133, 137-38, 141, 145, 147-48
Participative management 122
Pay incentive 125-26
Perception 105, 113, 150
Performance 16, 39, 53, 56, 75, 81, 87, 89, 93, 96, 118, 138, 144, 146
Personal Relations Survey 140
Planned change 5, 16, 125-27, 130
Politics of change 32
Porter Job Satisfaction Questionnaire 118
Power 21, 29, 44, 59, 67, 112
  equalization of 77
  redistribution of 53, 76

structure of 76
Prestige 44
Primary mentality 43
Problem Analysis Questionnaire 107, 113
Problem Expression Scale 103
Problem solving 14, 17, 21-22, 30, 32-33, 43, 48, 61, 66, 73, 82, 85, 89, 106, 112, 117, 124, 133, 136, 138, 140, 145
Process 38, 42, 85, 88, 112
  analysis 117
  consultation 11, 34, 80, 85, 99, 107
  work 59
Productivity 15, 40, 138, 144
Profit 44
Protest 59
Psychological health 19
Public service organizations 142
Punishment 81. See also Behavioral change; Reinforcement

Q

Q-sort 38

R

Refreezing 24, 43, 115
Regression 19, 117
Reinforcement 81. See also Behavioral change; Punishment
Research designs 24, 38, 47, 71, 75
Researcher 70
Resistance to change 3, 5, 9, 11, 16, 18, 22-24, 27, 35-37, 40, 45, 47-48, 52, 54, 61-62, 70, 96, 120, 138, 140-42. See also Support for change
Responsibility 119
Reward system 39, 56, 73, 81, 125. See also Behavioral change
Risk and risk taking 43-44, 54, 59, 84, 107, 144
Role 6-7, 11, 18, 22, 34, 38, 53, 63-64, 66, 71, 84, 91, 115, 122, 128, 141
  elaboration 38
  playing 8, 21, 149
  prescription 38

MAR 15 1979